Shipwreck

THE COAST OF UTOPIA PART II

Tom Stoppard's other work includes *Enter a Free Man*, *Rosencrantz and Guildenstern Are Dead*, *The Real Inspector Hound*, *Jumpers*, *Travesties*, *Night and Day*, *Every Good Boy Deserves Favour* (with Andre Previn), *After Magritte*, *Dirty Linen*, *The Real Thing*, *Hapgood*, *Arcadia*, *Indian Ink* and *The Invention of Love*. His radio plays include: *If You're Glad, I'll Be Frank*, *Albert's Bridge*, *Where Are They Now?*, *Artist Descending a Staircase*, *The Dog It Was That Died* and *In the Native State*. Work for television includes *Professional Foul* and *Squaring the Circle*. His film credits include *Empire of the Sun*, *Rosencrantz and Guildenstern Are Dead*, which he also directed, *Shakespeare in Love* (with Marc Norman) and *Enigma*.

TOM STOPPARD

Shipwreck

THE COAST OF UTOPIA
PART II

faber and faber

First published in hardback and paperback in 2002
by Faber and Faber Limited
3 Queen Square London WC1N 3AU

Typeset by Country Setting, Kingsdown, Kent CT14 8ES
Printed in England by Mackays of Chatham plc, Chatham, Kent

A CIP record for this book
is available from the British Library

ISBN
0–571–21662–5 (hbk)
0–571–21663–3 (pbk)

2 4 6 8 10 9 7 5 3 1

I am gratefully indebted to Trevor Nunn
for encouraging me towards some additions
and subtractions while *The Coast of Utopia*
was in rehearsal

Acknowledgements

I would like to thank, first, Aileen Kelly, who has written extensively about Alexander Herzen and Mikhail Bakunin. I am indebted to her for her kindness as well as her scholarship. Moreover, Dr Kelly is, with Henry Hardy, who also has my gratitude for our exchanges, the co-editor of the book which was my entry to the world of *The Coast of Utopia*, namely *Russian Thinkers*, a selection of essays by Isaiah Berlin. Berlin is one of two authors without whom I could not have written these plays, the other being E. H. Carr, whose *The Romantic Exiles* is in print again after nearly seventy years, and whose biography of Bakunin deserves to be. I received valuable help from Helen Rappaport on Russian matters in general. I am particularly indebted to her for Russian translation, including lines of dialogue. Krista Jussenhoven kindly made up my deficiency in German, Rose Cobbe corrected my French, and Sonja Nerdrum supplied me with the lines in Italian. My thanks to all of them, and to the Royal National Institute for the Deaf for access to its library.

Shipwreck was first performed in the Olivier auditorium of the National Theatre, London, as the second part of *The Coast of Utopia* trilogy, on 8 July 2002. The cast was as follows:

Nicholas Ogarev Simon Day
Natalie Herzen Eve Best
Ivan Turgenev Guy Henry
Sasha Herzen Lewis Crutch/Freddie Hale/
   Thomas Moll/Greg Sheffield
Nurse Janet Spencer-Turner
Alexander Herzen Stephen Dillane
Timothy Granovsky Iain Mitchell
Nicholas Ketscher Paul Ritter
Konstantin Aksakov Sam Troughton
Policeman Richard Hollis
Vissarion Belinsky Will Keen
Madame Haag Janine Duvitski
Kolya Herzen Padraig Goodall/Matthew Thomas-Davies/
   David Perkins
George Herwegh Raymond Coulthard
Emma Herwegh Charlotte Emmerson
Nicholas Sazonov Jonathan Slinger
Jean-Marie Thomas Arnold
Michael Bakunin Douglas Henshall
Karl Marx Paul Ritter
Shop Boy Dominic Barklem/Alexander Green/
   William Green/Ashley Jones
Natalie (Natasha) Tuchkov Lucy Whybrow
Benoit Martin Chamberlain

Blue Blouse John Nolan
Maria Ogarev Felicity Dean
Franz Otto Paul Ritter
Rocca Jack James
Tata Herzen Clemmie Hooton/Alice Knight/
    Harriet Lunnon/Casi Toy
Maria Fomm Anna Maxwell Martin
Leonty Ibayev John Carlisle
Other parts played by Rachel Ferjani, Jasmine Hyde,
    Sarah Manton, Jennifer Scott Malden, Nick Sampson,
    Kemal Sylvester, David Verrey

Director Trevor Nunn
Set, Costume and Video Designer William Dudley
Lighting Designer David Hersey
Associate Director Stephen Rayne
Music Steven Edis
Movement Director David Bolger
Sound Designer Paul Groothuis
Company Voice Work Patsy Rodenburg

Characters

Alexander Herzen, *a radical writer*
Natalie Herzen, *Alexander's wife*
Tata Herzen, *the Herzens' daughter*
Sasha Herzen, *the Herzens' son*
Kolya Herzen, *the Herzens' younger son*
Nicholas Ogarev, *a poet and radical*
Ivan Turgenev, *a poet and writer*
Timothy Granovsky, *a historian*
Nicholas Ketscher, *a doctor*
Konstantin Aksakov, *a Slavophile*
Nurse, *a household serf*
Policeman
Vissarion Belinsky, *a literary critic*
George Herwegh, *a radical poet*
Emma Herwegh, *his wife*
Madame Haag, *Herzen's mother*
Nicholas Sazonov, *a Russian émigré*
Michael Bakunin, *a Russian émigré activist*
Jean-Marie, *a French servant*
Karl Marx, *author of* The Communist Manifesto
Shop Boy
Natalie (Natasha) Tuchkov, *Natalie's friend*
Benoit, *a French servant*
Blue Blouse, *a Paris worker*
Maria Ogarev, *Ogarev's estranged wife*
Franz Otto, *Bakunin's defence lawyer*
Rocca, *an Italian servant*
Maria Fomm,. *a German nanny*
Leonty Ibayev, *Russian Consul in Nice*

The action takes place between 1846 and 1852 at Sokolovo, a gentleman's estate fifteen miles outside Moscow; Salzbrunn, Germany; Paris; Dresen; and Nice

SHIPWRECK

Act One

SUMMER 1846

The garden of Sokolovo, a gentleman's estate fifteen miles outside Moscow.

Nicholas Ogarev, aged thirty-four, has been reading to Natalie Herzen, aged twenty-nine, from a so-called 'thick journal', the Contemporary. *Ivan Turgenev, aged twenty-eight, is supine, out of earshot, with his hat over his face.*

Natalie Why have you stopped?

Ogarev I can't read any more. He's gone mad. (*He closes the book and lets it fall.*)

Natalie Well, it was boring anyway.

Sasha Herzen, aged seven, runs across the garden followed by a Nurse pushing a baby carriage. Sasha has a fishing cane and a jar for tiddlers.

Sasha, not too close to the river, darling! – (*to the Nurse*) Don't let him play on the bank!

The Nurse follows Sasha out.

Ogarev But . . . it was a fishing rod, wasn't it?

Natalie (*calling*) And where's Kolya? – (*looking aside*) Oh, all right, I'll keep an eye. (*resuming*) I don't mind being bored, especially in the country, where it's part of the attraction, but a boring book I take personally. (*looking aside, amused*) Far better to spend the time eating marigolds. (*glancing at Turgenev*) Has he gone to sleep?

3

Ogarev He didn't say anything about it to me.

Natalie Alexander and Granovsky will be back from picking mushrooms soon . . . Well, what should we talk about?

Ogarev Yes . . . by all means.

Natalie Why does it feel as though one has been here before?

Ogarev Because you were here last year.

Natalie But don't you ever have the feeling that while real time goes galloping down the road in all directions, there are certain moments . . . situations . . . which keep having their turn again? . . . Like posting stations we change horses at . . .

Ogarev Have we started yet? Or is this before we start talking about something?

Natalie Oh, don't be sideways. Anyway, something's wrong this year . . . even though it's all the same people who were so happy together when we took the house last summer. Do you know what's different?

Ogarev I wasn't here last summer.

Natalie No, it's not that. Ketscher's gone into a sulk . . . grown men squabbling over how to make coffee . . .

Ogarev But Alexander was right. The coffee is not good, and perhaps Ketscher's method will improve it.

Natalie Oh, I'm sure it's not like Parisian coffee! . . . Perhaps you're wishing you'd stayed in Paris.

Ogarev No. Not at all.

Turgenev stirs.

Natalie Ivan . . .? He's in Paris anyway, dreaming about the Opera!

Ogarev Yes, I'll say one thing, Viardot can sing.

Natalie But she's so ugly.

Ogarev Anyone can love a beauty. Turgenev's love for his opera singer is a reproach to us for batting the word about like a shuttlecock. (*Pause.*) When Maria wrote to introduce herself to you and Alexander after we got married, she described herself as ugly. I'm paying myself a compliment.

Natalie She also wrote that she had no vanity and loved virtue for its own sake . . . She was no judge of her looks either, forgive me, Nick.

Ogarev (*tolerantly*) Well, if we're talking about love . . . Oh, the letters one wrote . . . 'Ah, but to love you is to love God and His Universe, our love negates egoism in the embrace of all mankind.'

Natalie We all wrote that – why not? – it was true.

Ogarev I remember I wrote to Maria that our love would be a tale told down the ages, preserved in memory as a sacred thing, and now she's in Paris living quite openly with a mediocre painter.

Natalie That's a different thing – one might say a normal coaching accident – but at least you had each other body and soul before the coach went into the ditch. Our friend here simply trails along in Viardot's dust shouting *brava*, *bravissima* for favours forever withheld . . . not to mention her husband, the postillion.

Ogarev Are you sure you wouldn't rather talk about highway travel?

Natalie Would that be less painful for you?

Ogarev For me it's the same thing.

Natalie I love Alexander with my whole life, but it used to be better, when one was ready to crucify a man or be crucified for him for a word, a glance, a thought . . .
I could look at a star and think of Alexander far away in exile looking at the same star, and feel we were . . . you know . . .

Ogarev (*pause*) Triangulated.

Natalie Foo to you, then.

Ogarev (*surprised*) Believe me, I . . .

Natalie Now grown-upness has caught up with us . . . as if life were too serious for love. The wives disapprove of me, and it didn't help that Alexander's father died and left him quite rich. Duty and self-denial are the thing among our group.

Ogarev Duty and self-denial restrict our freedom to express our personality. I explained this to Maria – she got it at once.

Natalie Well, she didn't love you properly. I know I love Alexander, it's just that we're not the intoxicated children we were when we eloped in the dead of night and I didn't even bring my hat . . . And there was that other thing, too . . . He told you. I know he told you.

Ogarev Oh, well, yes . . .

Natalie I suppose you're going to say it was only a servant girl.

Ogarev No, I wouldn't say that. 'Only a countess' is more the line I take on these things.

Natalie Well, it put an end to stargazing, and I'd never have known if Alexander hadn't confessed it to me . . . Men can be so stupid.

Ogarev It's funny, though, that Alexander, who goes on about personal freedom, should feel like a murderer because on a single occasion, arriving home in the small hours, he . . .

Turgenev stirs and raises his head.

(*adjusting*) . . . travelled without a ticket . . .

Turgenev relapses.

. . . changed horses, do I mean? – no, sorry . . .

Turgenev sits up, taking the creases out of himself. He is somewhat dandified in his dress.

Turgenev Is it all right for him to eat them?

Natalie looks quickly toward Kolya but is reassured.

Natalie (*calls*) Kolya! (*then leaving*) Oh, he's getting so muddy! (*Natalie leaves.*)

Turgenev Have I missed tea?

Ogarev No, they're not back yet.

Turgenev I shall go in search.

Ogarev Not that way.

Turgenev In search of tea. Belinsky told me a good story I forgot to tell you. It seems some poor provincial schoolmaster heard there was a vacancy in one of the Moscow high schools, so he came up to town and got an interview with Count Strogonov. 'What right have you to this post?' Strogonov barked at him. 'I ask for the post,' said the young man, 'because I heard it was vacant.' 'So is the ambassadorship to Constantinople,' said Strogonov. 'Why don't you ask for that?'

Ogarev Very good.

Turgenev And the young man said –

Ogarev Oh.

Turgenev 'I had no idea it was in Your Excellency's gift, I would accept the post of ambassador to Constantinople with equal gratitude.' (*Turgenev laughs loudly by himself. He has a light high voice, surprising in one of his frame, and a braying laugh.*) Botkin's taken up a collection to send Belinsky to a German spa . . . doctor's orders. If only my mother would die, I'd have at least twenty thousand a year. Perhaps I'll go with him. The waters might reassure my bladder. (*He picks up the* Contemporary.) Have you read what Gogol's got in here? You could wait till the book comes out . . .

Ogarev If you ask me, he's gone mad.

Natalie returns, wiping soil from her hands.

Natalie I call to him as if he can hear me. I still think one day I'll say 'Kolya!' and he'll turn his face to me. (*She wipes a tear with her wrist.*) What do you think he thinks about? Can he have thoughts if he has no names to go with them?

Turgenev He's thinking muddiness . . . flowerness, yellowness, nice-smellingness, not-very-nice-tastingness . . . The names for things don't come first, words stagger after, hopelessly trying to become the sensation.

Natalie How can you say that – you, a poet?

Ogarev That's how we know.

Turgenev turns to Ogarev, silenced and deeply affected.

Turgenev (*pause*) I thank you. As a poet. I mean, you as a poet. I myself have started writing stories now. (*Turgenev starts to leave towards the house.*)

Ogarev I like him. He's not so affected as he used to be, do you think?

Turgenev returns, a little agitated.

Turgenev You don't understand Gogol, if I may say so. It's Belinsky's fault. I love Belinsky and owe a great deal to him, for his praise of my first poem, certainly, but also for his complete indifference to all my subsequent ones – but he browbeat us into taking Gogol as a realist . . .

Alexander Herzen, aged thirty-four, and Granovsky, aged thirty-three, approach, Herzen with a basket.

Natalie (*jumps up*) They're here . . . Alexander!

She embraces Herzen as warmly as decorum allows her.

Herzen My dear . . . but what's this? We haven't come from Moscow.

Granovsky goes unsmilingly towards the house.

Natalie Have you been quarrelling?

Herzen Disputing. He'll get over it. The only trouble is, we were having such an interesting talk . . .

He turns the basket upside down, letting a single mushroom fall out.

Natalie Oh, Alexander! I can see one from *here*!

She snatches the basket and runs off with it. Herzen takes her chair.

Herzen What were you and Natalie saying about me? Well, thank you very much, anyway.

Ogarev What were you and Granovsky arguing about?

Herzen The immortality of the soul.

Ogarev Oh, that.

Ketscher, aged forty, a thin, avuncular figure to the younger men, comes from the house carrying, with a slightly ceremonial air, a tray with a coffee pot on a small spirit lamp, and cups. In silence Herzen, Ogarev and Turgenev watch him put the tray on a garden table and pour a cup, which he brings to Herzen. Herzen sips the coffee.

Herzen It's the same.

Ketscher What?

Herzen It tastes the same.

Ketscher So you think the coffee is no better?

Herzen No.

The others are now nervous. Ketscher gives a short barking laugh.

Ketscher Well, it really is extraordinary, your inability to admit you're wrong even on such a trifling matter as a cup of coffee.

Herzen It's not me, it's the coffee.

Ketscher No, I mean it's beyond anything, this wretched vanity of yours.

Herzen I didn't make the coffee, I didn't make the coffee pot, it's not my fault that –

Ketscher To hell with the coffee! You're impossible to reason with! It's over between us. I'm going back to Moscow! (*Ketscher leaves.*)

Ogarev Between the coffee and the immortality of the soul, you'll end up with no friends at all.

Ketscher returns.

Ketscher Is that your last word?

Herzen takes another sip of coffee.

Herzen I'm sorry.

Ketscher Right.

Ketscher leaves again, passing Granovsky entering.

Granovsky (*to Ketscher*) How's the . . .? (*Seeing Ketscher's face, Granovsky lets the matter drop.*) Aksakov's in the house.

Herzen Aksakov? Impossible.

Granovsky (*helping himself to coffee*) Just as you like. (*He makes a face at the taste of the coffee.*) He's ridden over from some friends of his . . .

Herzen Well, why doesn't he come out? There's no need for old friends to fall out over . . .

Ketscher returns as though nothing had passed. He pours himself coffee.

Ketscher Aksakov's come. Where is Natalie?

Herzen Picking mushrooms.

Ketscher Ah . . . good. I must say they were excellent at breakfast. (*He sips his coffee while the others watch him, and considers it.*) Vile. (*He puts the cup down and, in a flurry, he and Herzen are kissing each other's cheeks and clasping each other, competing in self-blame.*)

Ketscher By the way, did I tell you, we're all going to be in the dictionary?

Herzen I'm already in the dictionary.

Granovsky He doesn't mean the German dictionary, in which you make a singular appearance, Herzen, and only by accident . . .

Ketscher No, I'm talking about a new word altogether.

Herzen Excuse me, Granovsky, but I wasn't an accident, I was the child of an affair of the heart, given my surname for my mother's German heart. Being half-Russian and half-German, at heart I'm Polish, of course . . . I often feel quite partitioned, sometimes I wake up screaming in the night that the Emperor of Austria is claiming the rest of me.

Granovsky That's not the Emperor of Austria, it's Mephistopheles, and he is.

Turgenev laughs.

Ogarev What's the new word, Ketscher?

Ketscher You can whistle for it now. (*furiously to Herzen*) Why do you feel you have to make off with every conversation like a bag-snatcher?

Herzen (*protesting, to Ogarev*) I don't, do I, Nick?

Granovsky Yes, you do.

Ketscher (*to Granovsky*) It's you as well!

Herzen In the first place, I have a right to defend my good name, not to mention my mother's. In the second place –

Ogarev Stop him, stop him!

Herzen joins in the laughter against himself.
Aksakov, aged twenty-nine, comes from the house.
He seems to be in costume. He wears an embroidered side-fastening shirt and a velvet skullcap. His trousers are tucked into tall boots.

Herzen Aksakov! Have some coffee!

Aksakov (*formally*) I wanted to tell you in person that relations are over between us. It's a pity, but there is no help for it. You understand that we can no longer meet as friends. I want to shake you by the hand and say goodbye.

Herzen allows his hand to be shaken. Aksakov starts to walk back.

Herzen What is the matter with everybody?

Ogarev Aksakov, why do you dress like that?

Aksakov (*turning angrily*) Because I am proud to be Russian!

Ogarev But people think you're a Persian.

Aksakov I have nothing to say to you, Ogarev. As a matter of fact, I don't hold it against you compared with some of your friends who spend their time gallivanting around Europe . . . because I understand that in your case you're not chasing after false gods but only after a false –

Ogarev (*hotly*) You be careful, sir, or you will hear from me!

Herzen (*leaping in*) That's enough of that talk! –

Aksakov You Westernisers apply for passports with letters from your doctors and then go off and drink the waters in Paris . . .

Ogarev relapses, seething.

Turgenev (*mildly*) Not at all, not at all. You can't drink the water in Paris.

Aksakov Go to France for your cravats if you must, but why do you have to go to France for your ideas?

Turgenev Because they're in French. You can publish anything you like in France, it's extraordinary.

Aksakov And what's the result? Scepticism. Materialism. Triviality.

Ogarev, still furious and agitated, leaps up.

Ogarev Repeat what you said!

Aksakov Scepticism – materialism –

Ogarev Before!

Aksakov Censorship is not all bad for a writer – it teaches precision and Christian patience.

Ogarev (*to Aksakov*) Chasing after a false what?

Aksakov (*ignoring*) France is a moral cesspit but you can publish anything you like, so you're all dazzled – blinded to the fact that the western model is a bourgeois monarchy for philistines and profiteers.

Herzen Don't tell me, tell them.

Ogarev goes out.

Aksakov (*to Herzen*) Oh, I've heard about your socialist utopianism. What use is that to us? This is Russia . . . (*to Granovsky*) We haven't even got a bourgeoisie.

Granovsky Don't tell me, tell him.

Aksakov It's all of you. Jacobins and German sentimentalists. Destroyers and dreamers. You've turned your back on your own people, the real Russians abandoned a hundred and fifty years ago by Peter the Great Westerniser! – but you can't agree on the next step.

Ogarev enters.

Ogarev I demand that you finish what you were going to say!

Aksakov I'm afraid I can't remember what it was.

Ogarev Yes, you can!

Aksakov A false beard . . .? No . . . A false passport . . .?

Ogarev goes out.

We have to reunite ourselves with the masses from whom we became separated when we put on silk breeches and powdered wigs. It's not too late. From our village communes we can still develop in a Russian way, without socialism or capitalism, without a bourgeoisie, yes, and with our own culture unpolluted by the Renaissance, and our own Church unpolluted by the Popes or by the Reformation. It can even be our destiny to unite the Slav nations and lead Europe back to the true path. It will be the age of Russia.

Ketscher You've left out our own astronomy unpolluted by Copernicus.

Herzen Why don't you wear a peasant's shirt and bast shoes if you want to advertise the real Russia, instead of dressing it up like you in your costume? Russia before Peter had no culture. Life was ugly, poor and savage. Our only tradition was submitting ourselves to invaders. The history of other nations is the history of their emancipation. The history of Russia goes the opposite way, to serfdom and obscurantism. The Church of your infatuated icon-painter's imagination is a conspiracy of pot-house priests and anointed courtiers in trade with the police. A country like this will never see the light if we turn our backs to it, and the light is over there. (*He points.*) West. (*He points the other way.*) There is none there.

Aksakov Then you that way, we this way. Farewell.

Leaving, Aksakov meets Ogarev storming in.

We lost Pushkin – (*He 'shoots' with his finger.*) – we lost Lermontov. (*He 'shoots' again.*) We cannot lose Ogarev. I ask your forgiveness.

He bows to Ogarev and leaves. Herzen puts his arm around Ogarev.

Herzen He's right, Nick.

Granovsky It's not the only thing he's right about.

Herzen Granovsky . . . let's not be quarrelling when Natalie comes back.

Granovsky I'm not quarrelling. He's right about us having no ideas of our own, that's all.

Herzen Where would they come from when we have no history of thought, when nothing has been handed on because nothing can be written or read or discussed? No wonder Europe regards us as a barbarian horde at the gates. This huge country, so vast it takes in fur-trappers, camel-herders, pearl-fishers . . . and yet not a single original philosopher, not one contribution to political discourse . . .

Ketscher Yes – one! The intelligentsia!

Granovsky What's that?

Ketscher It's the new word I was telling you about.

Ogarev Well, it's a horrible word.

Ketscher I agree, but it's our own, Russia's debut in the lexicon.

Herzen What does it mean?

Ketscher It means us. A uniquely Russian phenomenon, the intellectual opposition considered as a social force.

Granovsky Well . . .!

Herzen The . . . intelligentsia! . . .

Ogarev Including Aksakov?

Ketscher That's the subtlety of it, we don't have to agree with each other.

Granovsky The Slavophiles are not entirely wrong about the West, you know.

Herzen I'm sure they're entirely right.

Granovsky Materialism . . .

Herzen Triviality.

Granovsky Scepticism above all.

Herzen Above all. I'm not arguing with you.

Granovsky But – don't you see? – it doesn't follow our own bourgeoisie has to adopt the same values as in the West.

Herzen No. Yes.

Granovsky How would you know, anyway?

Herzen I wouldn't. It's you and Turgenev who've been there. I still can't get a passport. I've applied again.

Ketscher For your health?

Herzen (*laughs*) It's for little Kolya . . . Natalie and I want to consult the best doctors . . .

Ogarev (*looking*) Where is Kolya . . .?

Ketscher I'm a doctor. He's deaf. (*Shrugs.*) I'm sorry.

Ogarev, unheeded, leaves to look for Kolya.

Turgenev It's not all philistines, either. The only thing that'll save Russia is western culture transmitted by . . . people like us.

Ketscher No, it's the Spirit of History, the ceaseless March of Progress . . .

Herzen (*venting his anger*) Oh, a curse on your capital letters! We're asking people to spill their blood – at least spare them your conceit that they're acting out the biography of an abstract noun!

Ketscher Oh, it's my conceit? (*to the others*) There was nothing wrong with that coffee, either.

Herzen (*to Granovsky, conciliatory*) I'm not starry-eyed about France. To sit in a café with Louis Blanc, Leroux, Ledru-Rollin . . . to buy *La Réforme* with the ink still wet, and walk in the Place de la Concorde . . . the thought excites me like a child, I admit that, but Aksakov is right – I don't know the next step. Where are we off to? Who's got the map? We study the ideal societies . . . power to the experts, to the workers, to the philosophers . . . property rights, property sanctions, the evil of competition, the evil of monopoly . . . central planning, free housing, free love . . . limited to eight hundred families or unconstrained by national frontiers . . . and all of them uniquely harmonious, just and efficient. But Proudhon is the only one who understands what the question is: why should anyone obey anyone else?

Granovsky Because that's what society means. You might as well ask, why should an orchestra play together? And yet, it can play together without being socialist.

Turgenev That's true! – my mother keeps an orchestra at Spasskoye. What I find even harder to grasp, however, is that she also owns the nightingales.

Herzen Bringing in Russia always seems to confuse things. I'm not saying socialism is history's secret plan, it just looks like the rational step.

Granovsky To whom?

Herzen To me. Not just me. The future is being scrawled on the factory walls of Paris.

Granovsky Why? Why necessarily? We have no factory districts. Why should we wait to be inundated from within by our very own industrialised Goths? Everything you hold dear in civilisation will be smashed on the altar of equality . . . the equality of the barracks.

Herzen You judge the common people after they've been brutalised. But people are good, by nature. I have faith in them.

Granovsky Without faith in something higher, human nature is animal nature.

Herzen Without superstition, you mean.

Granovsky Superstition? Did you say superstition?

Herzen forgets to keep his temper, and Granovsky starts to respond in kind until they are rowing.

Herzen Superstition! The pious and pitiful belief that there's something outside or up there, or God knows where, without which men can't find their nobility.

Granovsky Without 'up there', as you call it, scores have to be settled down here – that's the whole truth about materialism.

Herzen How can you – how dare you – throw away your dignity as a human being? You can choose well or badly without deference to a ghost! – you're a free man, Granovsky, there's no other kind.

Natalie arrives hurriedly and frightened. Her distress is at first misinterpreted. She runs to Alexander and hugs him, unable to speak. There are some mushrooms in her basket.

Natalie Alexander . . .

Herzen (*apologetically to Natalie*) It's only a little argument . . .

Granovsky (*to Natalie*) It grieves me deeply to have to absent myself from a household in which I have always received a kind welcome. (*Granovsky starts to leave.*)

Natalie There's a policeman come to the house – I saw him from the field.

Herzen A policeman?

A Servant comes from the house, overtaken by a uniformed Policeman.

Oh God, not again . . . Natalie, Natalie . . .

Policeman Is one of you Herzen?

Herzen I am.

Policeman You're to read this. From Count Orlov.

The Policeman gives Herzen a letter. Herzen tears it open.

Natalie (*to the Policeman*) I want to go with him.

Policeman I wasn't told . . .

Herzen hugs Natalie.

Herzen It's all right. (*Announces.*) After twelve years of police surveillance in and out of exile, Count Orlov has graciously let it be known, I can now apply to travel abroad . . .!

The others gather round him in relief and congratulation. The Policeman hesitates. Natalie snatches the letter.

Ketscher You'll see Sazonov again.

Granovsky He's changed.

Turgenev And Bakunin . . .

Granovsky He hasn't, I'm afraid.

Natalie '. . . to travel abroad to seek medical assistance in respect of your son Nikolai Alexandrovich . . .'

Herzen (*lifting her up*) Paris, Natalie!

Her basket of mushrooms falls and spills.

Natalie (*weeping with joy*) . . . Kolya! . . .(*Natalie runs off.*)

Herzen Where's Nick?

Policeman Good news, then.

Herzen takes the hint and tips him. The Policeman leaves.

Natalie (*returning*) Where's Kolya?

Herzen Kolya? I don't know. Why?

Natalie *Where is he?*

Natalie runs out, calling the name.

Herzen (*following hurriedly*) He can't hear you . . .

Turgenev rushes out after them, Granovsky and Ketscher following anxiously
   After a pause, during which Natalie can be heard distantly, silence falls.
   Distant thunder.

*Sasha enters from another direction, and turns to
look back. He comes forward and sees the spilled
mushrooms. He rights the basket.*
*Ogarev enters at peace, carrying Sasha's fishing
cane and jar, glancing behind him.*

Ogarev (*calls*) Come on, Kolya!

Sasha He can't hear you.

Ogarev Come along!

Sasha He can't hear you.

Ogarev goes back towards Kolya.
Distant thunder.

Ogarev There, you see? He heard that.

He goes out.
Sasha starts putting the mushrooms into the basket.

JULY 1847

Salzbrunn, a small spa town in Germany.
*[Belinsky and Turgenev took rooms on the ground
floor of a small wooden house in the main street. A
shack in the courtyard served them as a summer pavilion.]*
*Belinsky and Turgenev are reading separate manuscripts,
a short story and a long letter respectively, while drinking
water from large beakers. Belinsky is thirty-six and less
than a year from death. His face is pale and smooth. He
has a stout walking stick to hand.*
*Turgenev finishes first. He puts the letter on the table.
He waits for Belinksy to finish reading, and drinks from
his beaker, making a face. Belinsky finishes reading and
gives the manuscript to Turgenev. Turgenev waits for the
verdict. Belinsky nods thoughtfully, drinks from his beaker.*

22

Belinsky Hm. You don't tell the reader what *you* think.

Turgenev What *I* think? What has that got to do with the reader?

Belinsky laughs, coughs, slams his stick, recovers.

Belinsky And what do you think about my letter to Gogol?

Turgenev Oh . . . well, I don't see the necessity for it.

Belinsky Be careful, boy, or I'll stand you in the corner.

Turgenev You said what you had to say about his book in the *Contemporary*. Is this the future of criticism? – first the bad notice, then the abusive letter to the author?

Belinsky The censor cut at least a third of my review. But that's not the point. Gogol evidently thinks I rubbished his book because he took a swipe at me. I'm not having that. He has to be made to understand that I took personal offence *from cover to cover*! I loved that man. I *found* him. Now he's gone mad – and this apostle of Tsar Nicholas, this champion of serfdom, corporal punishment, censorship, ignorance and obscurantist piety, thinks I gave him a bad notice out of pique. His book is a crime against humanity and civilisation.

Turgenev No – it's a book . . . a bad, stupid book but with all the sincerity of religious mania – why drive him madder? You should pity him.

Belinsky thumps angrily with his stick.

Belinsky It's too important for pity. In other countries, the advance of civilised behaviour is everybody's business. In Russia, there's no division of labour, literature has to do it all. That was a hard lesson for me, boy. When I started off, I thought art was aimless, pure spirit. I was a young ruffian from the provinces, with the artistic

THE COAST OF UTOPIA

credo of a Parisian dandy. Remember Gautier? – 'Fools!
Cretins! A novel is not a pair of boots!'

Turgenev 'A sonnet is not a syringe! A play is not a
railway!'

Belinsky (*chiming with Turgenev*) 'A play is not a
railway!' Well, we have no railways, so that's another job
for literature, to open up the country. Are you laughing
at me, boy? I once heard a government minister say he
was against railways because they encouraged people
who should stay put to indulge in purposeless travel with
who knows what results. That's what we're up against.

Turgenev I'm not pure spirit, but I'm not society's
keeper either. No, listen, Captain! People complain about
me having no attitude in my stories. They're puzzled. Do
I approve or disapprove? Do I want the reader to agree
with this man or the other man? Whose fault is it that
this peasant is a useless drunkard, his or ours? What
about this story I gave you? – is the bailiff worse than
the master, or the master worse than the bailiff? Where
does the author stand? Why doesn't he come clean with
us? Well, maybe I'm wrong, but how would that make
me a better writer? What has it got to do with anything?
(*raising his voice*) Why are you getting at me anyway?
I'm not well, you know – well, I'm not not well like
you're not well – (*hastily*) – though you'll get better, don't
worry – sorry – but coming all this way to this dump to
keep you company . . . Can we not talk about art and
society with the waters sloshing through my kidneys? . . .

*Belinsky, who has been coughing, is suddenly in
distress. Turgenev comes to his aid.*

Easy, Captain! Easy . . .

Belinsky (*recovering*) The waters of Salzbrunn are not
the elixir of life in my opinion. It's a mystery how these

places get their reputation. Anyone can see they're killing people off like flies.

Turgenev Let's get out! Come with me to Berlin. I've got some friends going to London, I promised to see them off – or we can meet in Paris.

Belinsky No, I . . .

Turgenev You can't go home without seeing Paris!

Belinsky I suppose not.

Turgenev Are you all right now?

Belinsky Yes. (*He drinks some water.*)

Turgenev (*pause*) So you didn't like my story?

Belinsky Who said? You're going to be one of our great writers, one of the few – I'm never wrong.

Turgenev (*moved*) Oh . . . (*lightly*) You said Fenimore Cooper was as great as Shakespeare.

Belinsky That wasn't wrong, it was only ridiculous.

There is a transition.

JULY 1847

Paris. La Place de la Concorde.
   Turgenev and Belinsky are out walking. Belinsky stares gloomily around.

Turgenev Herzen has established himself in the Avenue Marigny. He's got a chandelier, and a footman to bring things in on a silver tray. The snow on his boots is all gone like *les neiges d'antan*. (*He points.*) The obelisk marks the spot where they had the guillotine.

Belinsky They say the Place de la Concorde is the most beautiful square in the world, don't they?

Turgenev Yes.

Belinsky Good. Well, I've seen it now. Let's walk back to where I saw that red-and-white dressing gown in the window.

Turgenev It was expensive.

Belinsky I only want to look at it.

Turgenev I'm sorry about . . . you know . . . going off to London like that.

Belinsky It's all right.

He coughs painfully.

Turgenev Are you getting tired? You wait here, I'll go to the cab rank.

Belinsky I could write amazing things in a dressing gown like that.

Turgenev leaves.

SEPTEMBER 1847

Belinsky recovers. A chandelier descends into view. Belinsky looks at it.

Herzen's voice makes him turn, as the stage – the room – fills simultaneously from different directions.

Turgenev is unwrapping a shopping parcel. Natalie has a bag of toys and books from a shop. Madame Haag, who is Herzen's mother and in her fifties, is in charge of Sasha and Kolya, who is technically aged four. Sasha is 'speaking' face to face with Kolya, saying 'Kol-ya, Kol-ya' with extra enunciation. Kolya has a spinning top.

*George Herwegh, aged thirty, a beautiful young man
with a feminine delicacy notwithstanding luxuriant facial
hair and beard, lies on a chaise, romantically exhausted,
having his brow dabbed with cologne by Emma, his
wife, who is blonde and handsome rather than pretty.
Sazonov, aged thirty-five, a gentleman down on his luck,
is in sympathetic attendance. A Nurse appears and
involves herself with Madame and the two children.
There is a Servant, a footman-valet, making himself
useful as a waiter.*

*In their dress, Herzen and Natalie have altered
strikingly, transformed into Parisians. Herzen's
previously combed-back hair and 'Russian' beard have
been stylishly barbered.*

*In the first part of the scene, there are separate
conversations going on. They take turns to occupy the
vocal foreground, but they are all continuous.*

Herzen You always look at my chandelier . . .

Turgenev (*about the parcel*) Can we see it? . . .

Sasha Kol-ya . . . Kol-ya . . .

Herzen . . . there's something about that chandelier . . .

Belinsky No . . . I was just . . .

Herzen . . . it makes my Russian friends uneasy. It says,
'Herzen is our first bourgeois worthy of the name! What
a loss to the intelligentsia!'

*The Servant offers a tray of titbits to Mother with an
aristocratic assurance.*

Servant Madame . . . may one tempt you?

Mother No . . .

Servant Of course. Perhaps later.

The Servant offers his tray here and there, then leaves.

Natalie Vissarion, look . . . look what I found in the toy shop . . .

Sasha Can I see?

Mother It's not for you, you've got toys of your own, too many.

Natalie is delayed by Mother.

(*upset*) I can't get used to your servant's manner.

Natalie Jean-Marie? But he has *beautiful* manners, Granny.

Mother That's what I mean – he behaves as if he's on equal terms, he makes *conversation* . . .

Turgenev reveals, from its tissue paper, a flamboyant silk robe with a large red design on white. He puts it on.

Turgenev Yes . . . yes, very nice You think you know somebody, and then it turns out you don't.

Belinsky (*embarrassed*) When I said Paris was a swamp of bourgeois greed and vulgarity, I meant apart from my dressing gown.

Natalie It's beautiful, you were right to get it. (*showing her shopping*) Now, see here, look – you can't go home without something for your daughter . . .

Belinsky Thank you . . .

Sasha Look, Kolya . . .

Natalie Leave it alone! Come on, out you go . . .
(*to Nurse*) *Prenez les enfants* . . .

Sasha (*to Belinsky*) They're all girls' things.

Belinsky Yes . . . I had a little boy, but he died.

Mother Come on, my lamb, let's go and see Tata . . . come, Sasha . . . a big boy like you, you want to play all the time . . .

Herzen Oh, let him be a child, *Maman.*

Turgenev takes off the dressing gown. Natalie takes it and wraps it loosely.

Natalie (*to Turgenev*) You've been in London?

Turgenev Just for a week.

Natalie Don't be mysterious.

Turgenev I'm not. Some friends of mine, the Viardots . . .

Natalie You went to hear Pauline Viardot sing?

Turgenev I wanted to see London.

Natalie (*laughs*) All right, then, tell me what London is like.

Turgenev Very foggy. Streets full of bulldogs . . .

Meanwhile, Mother, Sasha and Kolya negotiate their way out with the Nurse. Kolya leaves his top behind.
They encounter Bakunin entering. He is thirty-five, grandly bohemian. He greets Mother, kisses the children, and helps himself to a glass from the Servant's salver.

Bakunin The Russians are here! (*He kisses Natalie's hand.*) Natalie.

Herzen Bakunin. Who's with you?

Bakunin Annenkov and Botkin. We kept our cab – they've gone for two more.

Natalie Good – we're all going to the station.

Bakunin Sazonov! *Mon frère!* (*confidentially*) The green canary flies tonight – ten o'clock – usual place – pass it on.

Sazonov I told *you.*

Bakunin (*to George and Emma*) I knew George was here. I could smell eau de cologne in the street. You're supposed to drink it, you know, that's the whole thing about German water – (*to Belinsky*) You didn't waste your time in Salzbrunn dabbing it behind your ears, I hope. Turgenev! (*He draws Turgenev aside.*) This is the last thing I'll ever ask of you.

Turgenev No.

Belinsky Is it time to go?

Herzen Plenty of time.

Bakunin Belinsky! – Herzen says your letter to Gogol is a work of genius, he calls it your testament.

Belinsky That doesn't sound too hopeful.

Bakunin Listen, why go back to Russia ? The Third Section's got a cell all ready for you.

Natalie Stop it!

Bakunin Bring your wife and daughter to Paris. Think of it – you could publish free of censorship.

Belinsky That's enough to put anyone off.

Bakunin What are you talking about? You could publish your letter to Gogol and everyone would read it.

Belinsky It wouldn't mean anything . . . in this din of hacks and famous names . . . filling their columns every day with their bellowing and bleating and honking . . . it's like a zoo where the seals throw fish to the public.

None of it seems serious. At home the public look to writers as their real leaders. The title of poet or novelist really counts with us. Writers here, they think they're enjoying success. They don't know what success is. You have to be a writer in Russia, even one without much talent, even a critic . . . My articles get cut by the censor, but a week before the *Contemporary* comes out students hang around Smirdin's bookshop asking if it's arrived yet . . . and then they pick up every echo the censor missed, and discuss it half the night and pass copies around . . . If the writers here only knew, they'd pack their bags for Moscow and St Petersburg.

He is met with silence. Then Bakunin embraces him, and Herzen, mopping his eyes, does likewise.

Emma *Sprecht Deutsch, bitte!* [*Speak German, please!*]

Herzen, still moved, raises his glass to the room. The Russians soberly raise their glasses, toasting.

Herzen Russia. We know. They don't. But they'll find out.

The Russians drink the toast.

Bakunin And I never said goodbye to you when I left.

Belinsky We weren't speaking.

Bakunin Ah – philosophy! Great days!

Natalie (*to Belinsky*) Now, what about your wife?

Belinsky Cambric handkerchiefs.

Natalie That's not very romantic.

Belinsky Well, she's not.

Natalie Shame on you.

Belinsky She's a schoolteacher.

Natalie What's that got to do with it?

Belinsky Nothing.

Bakunin (*to Belinsky*) Well, I'll see you soon in St Petersburg.

Herzen How can you go home? You've been sentenced in absentia for *not* going home when they summoned you.

Bakunin You forget about the revolution.

Herzen What revolution?

Bakunin The Russian revolution.

Herzen I'm sorry, I haven't seen a paper today.

Bakunin The Tsar and all his works will be gone within a year, or two at the most.

Sazonov (*emotionally*) We were children of the Decembrists. (*to Herzen*) When you were arrested, by some miracle they overlooked me and Ketscher.

Herzen This is not a sensible conversation. There will have to be a European revolution first, and there's no sign of it. There's no movement among the people here. The opposition has no faith in itself. Six months ago meeting Ledru-Rollin or Louis Blanc in a café felt like being a cadet talking to veterans. Their superior condescension to a Russian seemed only proper. What had we got to offer? Belinsky's articles and Granovsky's lectures on history. But these celebrities of the left spend their time writing tomorrow's headlines and hoping that someone else will make the news to go with them. And don't they know what's good for us! Virtue by decree. They're building prisons out of the stones of the Bastille. There's no country in the world that has shed more blood for liberty and understands it less. I'm going to Italy.

Bakunin (*excitedly*) Forget about the French. Polish independence is the only revolutionary spark in Europe. I've been here six years and I know what I'm talking about. I'm in the market for a hundred rifles, by the way, payment in cash.

Sazonov shushes him urgently. The Servant has entered. He whispers to Bakunin.

My cabbie wants to go home. Can you lend me five francs?

Herzen No. You should have walked.

Turgenev I'll do it.

Turgenev gives five francs to the Servant, who leaves.

Belinsky Isn't it time to go?

Sazonov (*to Belinsky*) It's a shame. With your abilities you could have done more, instead of wasting your time in Russia.

Herzen (*to Sazonov*) And do tell us, what have *you* done? You don't think discussing the borders of Poland with the émigrés every day in the Café Lamblin is doing something? –

Sazonov Hold on, hold on, you forget our situation.

Herzen What situation? You've lived in freedom all these years, playing statesmen-in-waiting and calling yourselves pink budgerigars –

Sazonov (*furiously*) Who told you about the –

Herzen You did.

Sazonov (*bursting into tears*) I knew I wasn't to be trusted!

Emma *Parlez français, s'il vous plaît!*

33

Bakunin (*comforting Sazonov with a hug*) I trust you.

Natalie Is George all right?

Herzen I never saw a man more all right.

Natalie goes to George and Emma.

Bakunin (*to Herzen*) Don't be deceived by George Herwegh. He got expelled from Saxony for political activity.

Herzen Activity? George?

Bakunin And he's got what every revolutionary needs, a rich wife.

Herzen Nick Ogarev knew him when they were together in Paris . . . Nick gave me a letter . . .

Bakunin What's more, she'll do anything for him. I once heard Marx explaining economic relations to George for an hour while Emma rubbed his feet.

Herzen Why?

Bakunin He said his feet were cold . . . other parts of him, it seems, are kept warm by the Contesse d' Agoult.

Natalie (*to Emma*) Continuez, continuez . . .

Herzen (*offended*) I won't have tittle-tattle about my friends in my house . . . and anyway you don't know it's true.

Bakunin (*laughs*) You're right – maybe he's only boasting.

Emma continues to smooth George's brow.

Natalie (*arriving*) Ah, that's what love should be!

Bakunin Love is a mystery, and woman's privilege is to be the priestess of the mystery, vestal of the sacred flame.

Herzen Am I being reproached because I don't let you mother me?

Natalie I don't reproach you, Alexander, I only say it's a fine thing to see.

Herzen What is? George having the vapours?

Natalie No . . . a woman's love that transcends egoism.

Herzen Love without egoism cheats women of equality and independence, not to mention any other . . . satisfaction.

Bakunin He's right, madame!

Herzen But you just said the opposite!

Bakunin (*unabashed*) He's right again!

George (*in German*) Emma, Emma . . .

Emma *Was ist denn, mein Herz?* [*What is it, my precious?*]

George *Weiss ich nicht . . . Warum machst du nicht weiter?* [*I don't know . . . Why have you stopped?*]

    Emma resumes stroking his brow.

Natalie (*privately to Herzen*) You're being unkind.

Herzen I like George, but I'd feel ridiculous.

Natalie (*angrily*) Idealised love doesn't mean a lack of . . . or perhaps you think it does?

Herzen What's this?

Natalie It's despicable to imply George doesn't . . . satisfy a woman . . .

Herzen (*stung*) I'm sure he does – I'm told she's a countess.

Natalie I see. Well, if it's only a countess . . .

She leaves the room abruptly, leaving Herzen baffled. Belinsky is now on his knees on the floor, puzzling over some small flat wooden shapes, one of the toys. Bakunin loudly calls for attention.

Bakunin My friends! Comrades! I give you a toast! The liberty of each, for the equality of all!

There is a mild, dutiful attempt to repeat the toast.

Herzen What does that mean? It doesn't mean anything.

Bakunin I am not free unless you, too, are free!

Herzen That's nonsense. You were free when I was locked up.

Bakunin Freedom is a state of mind.

Herzen No, it's a state of not being locked up . . . of having a passport . . . I am devoted to you, Bakunin, I delight in the fanfare, no, the funfair of your pronouncements, I would name my child for you, but equally I would name you for my child, because everything which is simple you make difficult and everything difficult simple. You've made yourself a European reputation by a kind of revolutionary word-music from which it is impossible to extract an ounce of meaning, let alone a political idea, let alone a course of action. What freedom means is being allowed to sing in my bath as loudly as will not interfere with my neighbour's freedom to sing a different tune in his. But above all, let my neighbour and I be free to join or not to join the revolutionary opera, the state orchestra, the Committee of Public Harmony . . .

Turgenev This is a metaphor, is it?

Herzen Not necessarily.

Sazonov An orchestra is a very good metaphor. There is no contradiction between individual freedom and duty to the collective –

Herzen I'd like to be there when they play.

Sazonov – because being in the orchestra is the individual right.

Herzen We all missed it, Plato, Rousseau, Saint-Simon, me . . .

Bakunin The mistake is to put ideas before action. Act first! The ideas will follow, and if not – well, it's progress.

Herzen Belinsky – save me from this madness!

Belinsky I can't fit the pieces together to make a square – it's a children's puzzle and I can't do it . . .

Turgenev Perhaps it's a circle.

Natalie enters and hurries to Herzen, making it up with him.

Natalie Alexander . . .?

Herzen embraces her.

George *Mir geht es besser.* [*I feel better.*]

Belinsky Turgenev's got a point . . .

Emma *Georg geht es besser!* [*George is feeling better!*]

The dialogues which follow are written to be 'wasted'. They are spoken on top of each other, to make a continuum of word-noise.

Belinsky Our problem is feudalism and serfdom. What have these western models got to do with us? We're so big and backward!

Turgenev (*to Belinsky*) My mother's estate is ten times the size of Fourier's model society.

Belinsky I'm sick of utopias. I'm tired of hearing about them.

Simultaneously with the above dialogue:

Bakunin The Poles should go in with the Slavs. Nationalism is the only movement that's reached a revolutionary stage. A rising of all the Slav nations! Let me finish! Three necessary conditions – break up the Austrian Empire – politicise the peasants – organise the working class!

Sazonov (*talking over Bakunin*) Some of the Poles think you're a Tsarist agent. The French despise the Germans, the Germans distrust the French, the Austrians can't agree with the Italians, the Italians can't agree among themselves . . . but everybody hates the Russians.

Simultaneously with the above, the Servant enters to talk to Herzen.

Herzen (*to George*) *Du riechst wie eine ganze Parfumerie.* [*You smell like a perfume shop.*]

George *Wir haben der Welt Eau de Cologne und Goethe geschenkt.* [*Eau de cologne and Goethe, we gave to the world.*]

Servant (*to Herzen*) *Il y a deux messieurs en bas, Monsieur le Baron, qui retiennent deux fiacres.* [*There's two gentlemen downstairs, Baron, keeping on two cabs.*]

Herzen *Allez les aider à descendre leurs baggages.* [*Please help with the luggage.*]

Servant *Hélas, c'est mon moment de repos – c'est l'heure du café.* [*It's my time to go to the café, alas.*]

Herzen *Bien. C'est entendu.* [*Of course. I quite understand.*]

Servant *Merci, Monsieur le Baron.* [*Thank you, Baron.*]

The Servant leaves.

Natalie (*talking over the above*) And Heine!

Emma *Und Herwegh!*

Natalie Yes! Yes!

Emma *Du bist so bescheiden und grosszuegig. Schreibst du bald ein neues Gedicht?* [*You're so modest and generous. Are you going to write a new poem soon?*]

George *Ich hasse solche Fragen!* [*I hate you asking me that!*]

Emma *Verzeihg mir – sonst weine ich.* [*Forgive me – don't make me cry!*]

Kolya enters in search of his top.
   All the conversations cut off into silence simultaneously, but 'continue'.
   Turgenev and Belinsky are finally interrupted by Herzen (see reprise at end of Act One), signalling a general break-up and exodus, still 'silent'.
   Turgenev and Sazonov help Belinsky with his valise and parcels.
   Kolya is left alone.
   There is distant thunder, which Kolya doesn't hear. Then there is a roll of thunder nearer. Kolya looks around, aware of something.
   There is the growing sound of a roaring multitude, of rifle fire, shouting, singing, drumming . . . and a female voice, representing the famous actress Rachel, singing 'The Marseillaise'.
   Red banners and the Tricolour.

Natalie enters, picks up Kolya and takes him out.
[*The monarchy of Louis Philippe fell on 24 February 1848.*]

MARCH 1848

Exterior (Place de la Concorde).
[*Herzen's memoirs: These were the happiest days of Bakunin's life.*]
    Bakunin flourishes a huge red banner on a pole. He has just encountered Karl Marx, aged thirty. Marx is carrying a yellow-wrapped book, the Communist Manifesto. *Turgenev is gazing around in astonishment. A pigeon evidently excretes onto his head. He reacts.*

Bakunin Marx! Who'd have thought it?!

Marx It was bound to happen. I was expecting it.

Bakunin Why didn't you tell me? All our lives we'll remember where we were when France became a republic again!

Marx I was in Brussels, waiting for the first copy of the *Communist Manifesto* to come from the printer . . .

Bakunin I was in Brussels, too, waiting for *La Réforme* to arrive with my open letter to the French government . . .

Turgenev No! *I* was in Brussels! . . . *The Barber of Seville* . . . Can I have a look?

    Marx gives him the book.

Bakunin I've been on my feet twenty hours a day –

Marx Minister Flocon said that with three hundred more like you . . .

Bakunin . . . preaching rebellion, destruction . . .

Marx . . . France would be ungovernable.

Bakunin I've been living in barracks with the Republican Guard. You won't believe this but it's the first time I've actually met anyone from the working class.

Marx Really? What are they like?

Bakunin I've never come across such nobility.

Turgenev (*reading*) 'A ghost is going round Europe – the ghost of Communism!'

Bakunin A Polish National Committee has already been set up in Prussian Poland to plan the invasion of Russia. I've got to get there. Turgenev, this is the last thing I'll ever ask of you –

Turgenev Ask Flocon.

Bakunin You think the Provisional Government will give me the money to go to Poland?

Turgenev I'm certain of it.

Marx (*to Turgenev*) You're a writer. Do you think there's something funny about 'the ghost of Communism'? I don't want it to sound as if Communism is dead.

Herwegh enters in red, black and gold military uniform.

Bakunin Herwegh!

Marx (*to Turgenev*) Do you know English?

Turgenev Fairly well. Let me see . . . (*in 'English'*) 'A ghost . . . a phantom is walking around Europe . . .'

Herwegh (*somewhat embarrassed*) What do you think?

Bakunin Nice. Are you a mason?

Herwegh No – I'm in command of a brigade of German Democratic Exiles. We're going to march on Baden!

Bakunin March all the way to Germany?

Herwegh No, no, we're going to the frontier by train – I've got six hundred tickets.

Turgenev Did Flocon give you the money?

Herwegh Yes, how did you know?

Bakunin Wonderful!

Herwegh It was Emma's idea.

Turgenev I knew you weren't really a poet. Only a poet. Have you had any military experience?

Herwegh Emma says whether you're a poet or a revolutionary, genius is genius.

Bakunin She's right. Look at Byron.

Herwegh Byron wrote far too much, actually.

Turgenev returns to pondering the book. Emma enters. She, too, is in military mode, with a red, black and gold cockade. She is accompanied by a small boy in the livery of a fashionable store, who is burdened with elegantly wrapped parcels. He may have a small pushcart in the same livery.

Marx (*intervening sternly*) Just a moment, Herwegh!

Then Marx sees Emma.

Emma I've got provisions for the march, my angel – the most wonderful little meat pasties from Chevet, and a turkey stuffed with truffles –

Marx Scoundrel!

Emma He's got to eat, Karl. Come with us to the Champs Elysées – George is going to review the troops!

Marx is now beside himself with rage. He pursues the Herweghs out.

Marx Adventurist! By what right do you interfere in the economic struggle with this diversionary folly?

Emma Don't take any notice of him, darling.

Marx Victory in Europe will be decided between the proletariat and the bourgeoisie! – only ceaseless propaganda and agitation . . .

The shop boy follows Marx and the Herweghs out.

Turgenev (*thoughtfully*) 'A spook . . . a spectre . . .'

Bakunin (*transported*) This is what it was all for, from the beginning . . . studying Kant, Schelling, Fichte . . . with Stankevich, and Belinsky . . . with you in Berlin, do you remember, you in your lilac waistcoat, I in my green, walking down Unter den Linden talking furiously about the spirit of history . . .

Turgenev (*jogged*) 'A *spirit* . . . a spirit is haunting Europe . . .'

Bakunin We were on a journey to this moment. Revolution is the Absolute we pursued at Premukhino, the Universal which contains all the opposites and resolves them. It's where we were always going.

Turgenev (*taps the book, triumphantly satisfied*) 'A hobgoblin is stalking around Europe – the hobgoblin of Communism!'

He closes the book, looks up and 'shoots' twice.
Natalie and Natalie (Natasha) Tuchkov, aged nineteen, enter rapidly in high spirits. Natasha's hair

is wet. Natalie has a Tricolour wrapped round her as a shawl.

Natalie *Vive la République! Vive la République!*

The two women have entered the next scene.

15 MAY 1848

A different apartment, near the newly completed Arc de Triomphe. Herzen is with Kolya, holding Kolya's palms to his – Herzen's – face.

Herzen *Vive la République,* Kol-ya! (*to Natalie*) Where did you get that?

Natasha Everybody's wearing them!

Natalie and Natasha are in a state of ecstatic, romantic friendship in which everything is joyous or hilarious or soulful.

Natalie It's a present for you from Natasha.

Herzen Well . . . thank you.

Natalie removes the 'shawl' and presents it to Herzen, leaving herself déshabillée but only her shoulders and arms actually bare.

But you've got no clothes on.

Natasha I'm wearing them!

Natalie Poor darling, she arrived wet through, so I said –

Natasha 'Take off your clothes! At once!'

Natalie I made her put on my dress.

Herzen Of course. I had no idea you had only one dress. In fact, my impression was that you had a dress shop . . .

Natalie But I want her to smell of me, and I want to smell of her –

Natasha You smell like camellias . . .

Natalie inhales rapturously from Natasha's hair.

Natalie Russia!

Mother enters.

Mother Natalie! – suppose the servant came in . . .! (*taking Kolya*) Look at your terrible mother . . . If this is what goes on in a republic . . . (*to Natalie*) There's a letter for you.

Natasha It's from me!

Natalie and Natasha embrace.
Herzen drapes the flag over Natalie as a manservant, Benoit, opens the door to admit Sazonov with an air of condescension.

Sazonov *Citoyens!* – you're back at last . . .

Natalie and Natasha dash out past Sazonov, who is thrown off his stride. Benoit follows the women out.

And who was the young . . .?

Herzen (*lightly*) My wife has fallen in love . . . We met the family in Rome, they're neighbours of Ogarev back home.

Mother accepts Sazonov's bow.

Mother We arrived back ten days ago. (*to Kolya*) Come on, it's time for your and Tata's tea . . .

Herzen *Maman*, ask Benoit to post this for me, please . . .

He puts his written sheets into the prepared envelope and seals it.

Mother The Marquis? All right, but he's grander than the last one – the last one *spoke*, the new one always seems about to ask me to dance . . .

Mother leaves with Kolya, leaving behind Kolya's top.

Herzen French servants were the biggest surprise. I knew you weren't allowed to send them into the army or sell them . . . but nothing prepares you for their amazing efficiency, politeness and absolute lack of calling.

Sazonov Forget France! Don't you see? – our time has come. The Russian government is in an impasse. They won't want to be the pariahs of Europe. They'll have to make a gesture.

Herzen Oh, they will! They'll cancel all leave for the Cossacks, Tsar Nicholas will be the last righteous ruler in a wilderness of cowards and constitutions.

Sazonov No, *history is being made*! Russia is going to need a liberal cultured ministry, men with European experience. Have you thought of that?

Herzen I promise you, I never have.

Sazonov Well, the government will have to appeal to us.

Herzen You and me?

Sazonov Well, people of our circle.

Herzen (*laughs*) Which ministry do you fancy?

Sazonov You can laugh . . . but the stage is now bigger than your little articles for the *Contemporary*.

Herzen Nevertheless, the workers are marching on the National Assembly this morning . . . so let's see if the elected government acts like republicans . . .

There is a transition to some hours later, with a sound of rioting.
    Herzen enters tired and angry. Turgenev is shown in by Benoit.

(*to Benoit*) *Du vin.* [Wine.]

    Benoit leaves.

So, what do you think now of your democratic republic?

Turgenev Mine? I'm a tourist like you. You should be asking what the Parisians thought of it . . . and the remarkable thing is, you couldn't tell. It was as if they'd bought tickets and were interested to see how it would turn out. The lemonade and cigar sellers circulated, very content, like fishermen hauling in a good catch. The National Guard waited to see which way it was going, and then set about the mob.

Herzen The mob? Workers marching behind their banners.

Turgenev Invading the National Assembly to demand the self-abolition of an elected parliament which happens to be not to their taste.

Herzen Turgenev! – you talk to me of taste? A republic behaving like the monarchy it displaced is not a failure of aesthetics. This is a republic by superstition only, by incantation. *Vive la République!* But it turns out the Republic makes revolution unnecessary, and, in fact, undesirable. Power is not to be shared with the ignoramuses who built the barricades. They're too poor to have a voice.

Turgenev It was an insurrection, and order has triumphed

Herzen Well, don't imagine today was the end. When the lid blows off this kettle it'll take the kitchen with it.

All your civilised pursuits and refinements which you call the triumph of order will be firewood and pisspots once the workers kick down the doors and come into their kingdom. Do I regret it? Yes, I regret it. But we've enjoyed the feast, we can't complain when the waiter says, '*L'addition, messieurs!*'

Turgenev Goodness me . . . the sins of the Second Republic won't bear the weight of this revenge drama of cooks and waiters. The Provisional Government promised elections. Elections took place. Nine million Frenchmen voted for the first time. Well, they voted for royalists, rentiers, lawyers . . . and a rump of socialists for the rest to kick. You have a complaint? A coup d'état by the organised workers, and a salutary period of Terror, would put that right. You could be Minister of Paradox, with special responsibility for Irony. Herzen . . . Herzen! For all the venality you see around you, France is still the highest reach of civilisation.

Natalie and Natasha enter with George, who is shorn of his beard, moustache and dignity.

Herzen (*puzzled*) Yes . . . ?

Turgenev It's Herwegh, back from Germany.

Benoit follows with glasses of wine.

Herzen *Ach, mein armer Freund . . .* [*Oh, my dear fellow . . .*]

Natalie There was a price on his head!

Herzen embraces George, who bursts into tears.

Herzen *Trink einen Schluck Wein. Du bist ein Held!* [*Take some wine. You're a hero!*]

Herzen gives a glass to George. Turgenev, Natasha and Natalie take glasses from the salver.

(toasting) Auf die Revolution in Deutschland! [To the revolution in Germany!]

George *Dankeschoen, danke . . . [Thank you, thank you . . .] (toasting) Auf die Russische Revolution . . . und auf die Freundschaft! [To the Russian revolution . . . and to friendship!]*

Natalie To friendship!

Natasha And love!

Turgenev *(toasting) Vive la République!*

Herzen *(toasting) A bas les bourgeois! Vive le prolétariat!*

Benoit, leaving, registers pained reproach, just perceptibly.

Mille pardons, Benoit.

George weeps afresh. Natalie comforts him. There is a transition to a month later.

JUNE 1848

A 'Blue Blouse', an old workman in tattered clothes, stands in the room, a desperate motionless figure, invisible to Natalie and Natasha who, innocently embraced, recline on the couch, with George in attendance moping.

George Everybody's being horrible about me. They say I hid in a ditch as soon as the enemy came in sight. You don't believe it, do you?

Natalie Of course we don't.

Natasha Of course not.

Natalie Nor does Emma. Well, she was there.

George She pushed me into it.

Natalie The ditch?

George No, the whole business . . . chairman of the German democrats in exile, and suddenly I was Napoleon at Austerlitz.

Natasha Waterloo. Oh, sorry . . . but you looked so defeated.

George Emma still has faith in me. Perhaps she'll invade Poland. She was in love with me before she met me. So were half the women in Germany. My book of poems went through six editions. I met the King. Then I met Emma.

Natalie And she's the one who got you!

George I wish I'd listened to Marx.

Natalie Marx? Why?

George He tried to talk me out of it.

Natalie (*amazed*) Marrying Emma?

George No, the Legion of German Democrats.

Natalie Oh . . .!

George Now he's crowing over my humiliation . . . after all I've done for him, taking him to all the best houses, introducing him at Marie d'Agoult's salon . . .

Natasha The countess?

George Yes, the writer, one of my admirers.

Natalie And you were one of hers, surely . . . I admire her, too. When she fell in love with Liszt she followed her heart. Everything had to give way to love – reputation, society, husband, children . . . just like George Sand and Chopin! . . . Do you play?

George A little. I compose a bit, too. Emma says if I practised, Chopin and Liszt better watch out.

Natasha *Shto praiskhódit?* [*What's this?*]

Natalie (*to Natasha*) George looks like Onegin ought to look, don't you think? (*Natalie jumps up and pulls George by the hand.*) Come on, then!

Herzen enters.

George is going to play for us!

There is a distant sound of riot, and a transition. Herzen and the Blue Blouse remain.

Natasha (*to Natalie, warningly*) Natalie . . .

Natalie (*dissembling*) What?

Natasha You haven't got a piano.

Natalie (*brazenly*) Well?

The two women embrace hilariously and take George out.

Herzen sees the Blue Blouse.

Herzen What do you want? Bread? I'm afraid bread got left out of the theory. We are bookish people, with bookish solutions. Prose is our strong point, prose and abstraction. But everything is going beautifully. Last time – in 1789 – there was a misunderstanding. We thought we had discovered that social progress was a science like everything else. The First Republic was to have been the embodiment of morality and justice as a rational enterprise. The result was, admittedly, a bitter blow. But now there's a completely new idea. History itself is the main character of the drama, and also its author. We are all in the story, which ends with universal bliss. Perhaps not for you. Perhaps not for your children. But universal bliss, you can put your shirt on it which,

51

I see, you have. Your personal sacrifice, the sacrifice of countless others on History's slaughter-bench, all the apparent crimes and lunacies of the hour, which to you may seem irrational, are part of a much much bigger story which you probably aren't in the mood for – let's just say that this time, as luck would have it, you're the zig and they're the zag.

The noise of insurrection increases.

21 JUNE 1848

Street.

    [*From Turgenev's* Literary Reminiscences: '*At first there was nothing particular that I could see . . . But the farther I went the more did the appearance of the boulevard change. Carriages became less frequent, the omnibuses disappeared completely; the shops and cafés were being hastily closed . . . there were many fewer people in the street. On the other hand, all the windows of the houses were open, and a great number of people, mostly women, children, maids and nursemaids, were crowded in the doorways. They were all talking, laughing, not shouting but calling to one another, looking round, waving their hands – as though in expectation of some pageant. A light-hearted, festive curiosity seemed to have taken possession of people. Ribbons of many colours, kerchiefs, caps, white, pink, blue dresses shimmered and glittered, rose and rustled in the light summer breeze . . . The uneven line of the barricade, about eight feet high, came into sight. In the middle of it, surrounded by other tricolour and gold-embroidered banners, a small red flag fluttered with its ominous pointed tongue . . . I moved a little nearer. The space just in front of the barricade was almost deserted, only a few men walking to and fro in the roadway. The workers exchanged jokes with the spectators in the street who came up to them . . . One of them, with a white soldier's sword-belt round his waist, held out an uncorked bottle and a half-filled glass to them, as if inviting them to come up and have a drink; another, next to him, with a double-barrelled gun over his shoulder, yelled in a drawn-out voice, "Long live the democratic and socialist republic!" Beside him stood a black-haired woman in a striped dress, also with a sword-belt and a revolver thrust in it; she alone did not laugh . . . Meanwhile the sound of drums drew nearer and grew louder . . .'*]

Natalie, carrying Kolya, the Nurse pushing a stroller containing a three-year-old (Tata), as it were, and Mother holding Sasha's hand, hurry across the street. Sasha carries a Tricolour on a pole, which encumbers him.

Natalie Oh God – oh God – quickly . . . There were omnibuses full of corpses.

Mother You must be calm for the children . . .

Herzen meets them and takes Kolya.

Herzen (*to Sasha*) Go with Mama. What are you doing with that?

Sasha Benoit says to wave it for the Garde Mobile!

Herzen Go inside.

Natalie Did you see?

Herzen Yes.

Natalie The omnibuses?

Herzen Yes.

Rachel's voice is heard again . . . but 'The Marseillaise' is drowned out in volleys of rifle fire.

53

27 JUNE 1848

There is a transition to the interior, with cheerful music heard from the street.

Kolya remains with Herzen and sits on the floor with his top. Turgenev is with Herzen.

Benoit delivers some letters to Herzen on a salver, and leaves.

Turgenev Have you been out? It's amazing how life settles back. The theatres are open. There's carriages in the streets again, and ladies and gentlemen inspecting the ruins as if they were in Rome. To think it was only on Friday morning the laundress who brought my washing said, 'It's started!' And then four days shut away in this awful heat, listening to the guns, knowing what must be happening and helpless to do anything . . . oh, that was torture.

Herzen But with clean laundry.

Turgenev I trust if we're going to have this conversation –

Herzen I didn't invite conversation. If I were you, I'd take avoiding action. These four days could make one hate for a decade.

Turgenev I'll go, then. (*Pause.*) But allow me to express the opinion that somebody must do your laundry, too.

Herzen Letter from Granovsky! Just wait till he hears! (*He opens the letter.*) All you liberals are splashed with blood no matter how you tried to keep your distance. Yes, I have a laundress, possibly several, how would I know? The whole point of the serving class is that the rest of us, the fortunate minority, can concentrate on our higher destinies. Intellectuals must be allowed to think, poets to dream, landowners to own land, dandies to

54

perfect their cravats. It's a kind of cannibalism. The uninvited are necessary to the feast. I'm not a sentimental moralist. Nature, too, is merciless. So long as a man thinks it's the natural order of things for him to be eaten and for another to eat, then who should regret the death of the old order if not we who write our stories or go to the opera while others do our laundry? But once people realise the arrangement is completely artificial, the game is up. I take comfort in this catastrophe. The dead have exposed the republican lie. It's government by slogan for the sake of power, and if anyone objects there's always the police. The police are the realists in a pseudo-democracy. From one regime to the next, power passes down the system until it puts its thumbprint on every policeman's forehead like the dab of holy oil at an emperor's coronation. The conservatives can't keep the smiles off their faces, now they know the whole thing was a confidence trick. The liberals wanted a republic for their own cultivated circle. Outside it they're conservatives. They cheered on Cavaignac's butchers while wringing their hands with their fingers crossed. Well, now we know what the reactionaries have always known: liberty, equality and fraternity are like three rotten apples in their barrel of privilege, even a pip could prove fatal – from now on it's all or nothing, no quarter, no mercy.

Turgenev (*mildly*) You sound like Belinsky, adjusting some poet's reputation . . . Do you think there's something Russian about taking everything to extremes?

Herzen No doubt. Single-minded conviction is a quality of youth, and Russia is young. (*pointedly*) Compromise, prevarication, the ability to hold two irreconcilable beliefs, both with ironic detachment – these are ancient European arts, and a Russian who finds them irresistible is, I would say, exceptional.

Turgenev (*disingenuously*) How interesting that you should say that. Because I myself, you see –

Herzen, despite himself, laughs, and Turgenev laughs with him, but almost at once his laughter turns to anger.

Putting yourself in another's place is a proper modesty, and, yes, it takes centuries to learn it. Impatience, pigheaded stubbornness to the point of destruction – yes, these are things to be forgiven in the young, who lack the imagination to see that almost nothing in this life holds still, everything is moving and changing –

Herzen (*with Granovsky's letter, cries out*) Who is this Moloch who eats his children?

Turgenev Yes, and your taste for melodramatic, rhetorical –

Herzen Belinsky's dead.

Turgenev No, no . . . oh, no, no, no . . . No! . . . No more blather please. Blather, blather, blather. Enough.

Natalie enters and goes to Herzen.

Natalie Alexander . . . ?

SEPTEMBER 1847 (REPRISE)

Herzen, Natalie, Turgenev and Kolya remain, their positions corresponding to the reprised scene which now reassembles itself at the point of Natalie's re-entrance.

George *Mir geht es besser.* [*I feel better.*]

Belinsky Turgenev's got a point.

Emma *Georg geht es besser.* [*George is feeling better!*]

Belinsky Our problem is feudalism and serfdom.

*The rest of the scene now repeats itself with the differ-
ence that instead of the general babel which ensued,
the conversation between Belinsky and Turgenev is
now 'protected', with the other conversations virtually
mimed. At the point where the babel went silent
before, nothing now alters.*

What have these theoretical models got to do with us?
We're so big and backward!

Turgenev My mother's estate is ten times the size of
Fourier's model society.

Belinsky I'm sick of utopias. I'm tired of hearing about
them. I'd trade the lot for one practical difference that
owes nothing to anybody's ideal society, one common-
sensical action that puts right an injury to one person.
Do you know what I like to do best when I'm at home? –
watch them build the railway station in St Petersburg.
My heart lifts to see the tracks going down. In a year or
two, friends and families, lovers, letters, will be speeding
to Moscow and back. Life will be altered. The poetry
of practical gesture. Something unknown to literary
criticism! I'm sick of everything I've ever done. Sick of
it and from it. I fell in love with literature, and stayed
lovesick all my life. No woman had a more fervent or
steadfast adorer. I picked up every handkerchief she let
fall, lace, linen, snotrag, it made no difference. Every
writer dead or alive was writing for me personally, to
transport me, insult me, make me shout for joy or tear my
hair out, and I wasn't fooled often. Your *Sportsman's
Sketches* are the best thing since Gogol was young, and
this Dostoevsky is another if he can do it twice. People
are going to be amazed by Russian writers. In literature
we're a great nation before we're ready.

Turgenev You're going round again, Captain.

Herzen My god! We're going to miss it! (*comforting Natalie*) You're pale. Stay here. Stay with the children.

Natalie nods.

Natalie (*to Belinsky*) I won't come to the station. Have you got everything?

Bakunin It's not too late to change your mind.

Belinsky I know – it's my motto.

Natalie embraces Belinsky. Turgenev and Sazonov help Belinsky with his valise and his parcels.

Herzen Don't try to talk French. Or German. Just be helpless. Don't get on the wrong boat.

There is a general exodus, as before.
    Kolya is left alone.
    There are sounds of the cabs departing.
    There is distant thunder, which Kolya ignores. Then there is a roll of thunder nearer. Kolya looks around, aware of something.
    Natalie enters. She kisses Kolya on the nose, enunciating his name. He watches her mouth.

Natalie Kolya . . . Kolya . . .

Natalie notices Belinsky's dressing gown. She gives a cry of dismay and runs out of the room with it.

Kolya (*absent-mindedly*) Ko' ya . . . Ko' ya. (*He plays with his top.*)

Act Two

JANUARY 1849

Paris.

George has been reading to Herzen and Natalie.
Natalie sits with George at her feet. Herzen lies on the
couch with a silk handkerchief over his face. The book –
or booklet – is the Communist Manifesto *in its yellow*
wrapper.

Natalie Why have you stopped?

George closes the book and lets it fall. Natalie
smoothes George's hair.

George I don't see the point.

Natalie He's saying that all history up to now is the
history of class struggle. And by sheer luck, Marx himself,
the discoverer of this fact, is living in the very place, at
the very time, when, thanks to industrialisation, these
centuries of class struggle, from feudal times onwards –

George Yes, I've got that.

Natalie Well, then. It's all now arriving at the end of
history, with the final –

George But there's no point if every time you want to
argue back, Karl just says, 'Well you would think that,
because as a product of your class you can't think
anything else.' In my opinion, that's cheating.

Natalie I agree. But then I would, wouldn't I, because –

George You think what you are! You say, 'Karl, I don't
agree good and evil are to be defined *entirely* by our
economic relations,' and Karl replies –

Natalie 'Well, you would think that –'

George '– because you're not a member of the proletariat!'

Natalie and George delightedly clasp hands in mutual congratulation. Herzen removes the handkerchief from his face. Natalie continues to smooth George's hair.

Herzen But Marx is a bourgeois from the anus up.

Natalie Alexander! I won't have that word . . .

Herzen Sorry, middle-class.

George It's German genius, that's what it is.

Natalie What is?

George That if you're a miserable exploited worker, you're playing a vital role in a historical process that'll put you on top as sure as omelettes was eggs. Everything's functioning perfectly, you see! With the French geniuses, your miserable exploited no-accountness means there's a fault in the plumbing and they're here to fix it because you're too stupid to do it for yourself . . . So the workers have to hope the plumber knows what he's doing and won't cheat them. No wonder it didn't catch on.

Herzen But how can Communism catch on? It asks a worker to give up his . . . aristocracy. A cobbler with his own last is an aristocrat compared with the worker in a factory. A minimum of control over your own life, even to make a mess of it, is something necessarily human. What do you think goes wrong with those experimental societies? It's not the mosquitoes. It's something human refusing to erase itself. Still, at least Marx is an honest-to-God materialist. Those Marseillaise-singing orators

of the left won't let go of nurse. I feel sorry for them.
They're preparing for themselves a life of bewilderment
and grief . . . because the republic they want to bring
back is the last delirium of two thousand years of
metaphysics . . . the elavation of spirit over matter . . .
brotherhood before bread, equality by obedience,
salvation through sacrifice. To save this tepid bathwater,
they'll chuck out the baby and wonder where it went.
Marx gets it. We didn't get it – or we didn't have the
courage.

Natalie George risked his life on the field of battle!

Herzen So he did. You know, now that people have
started recognising you clean-shaven, you should grow
a beard.

Natalie You're a brute. (*to George*) He's only teasing.
Nobody cares about that any more, it's all forgotten.

Herzen I haven't forgotten.

Natalie Stop it.

George I don't mind. Would you like me to grow my
beard?

Natalie I've got used to you without it. What does
Emma say?

George She said I should ask you.

Natalie Oh! How flattering. But it's not me who gets the
tickles if you grow it back.

Herzen Why doesn't Emma come with you any more?

George I need to have an hour or two free from family
life. What an abominable institution.

Herzen I thought this was family life.

George Yes, but your wife is a saint. It's not Emma's fault. Her father was ruined by the dialectic of history, and he blames me. . . . It's very hard on Emma, losing her allowance. But what can I do? I'm a poet of revolution between revolutions.

Herzen takes up a few newly arrived letters and looks through them.

Herzen Write an ode to Prince Louis Napoleon on his election as President of the Republic. In a free vote, the French public renounced freedom.

George 'Bonaparte Plumbers, a name you can trust.'

Herzen How naive we were at Sokolovo that last summer in Russia, do you remember, Natalie?

Natalie I remember you quarrelling with everyone.

Herzen Arguing, yes. Because we were agreed that there was only one thing worth arguing about – France! France, the sleeping bride of revolution. What a joke. All she wanted was to be the kept woman of a bourgeois . . . Cynicism fills the air like ash and blights the leaves on the freedom trees.

Herzen gives one of the letters to Natalie.

Natalie Thank you . . . Oh, from Natasha! I miss her so, since she went home.

George One must learn to be a stoic. Look at me.

Herzen You're a stoic?

George What does it look like?

Herzen Apathy?

George Exactly. But apathy is misunderstood.

Herzen I'm very fond of you, George.

George *Apatheia!* To the ancient stoics there was nothing irresolute about apathy, it required strenuous effort and concentration.

Herzen *Very* fond of you.

George Because, being a stoic didn't mean a sort of uncomplaining putting-up with misfortune, that's only how it looks on the outside – inside, it's all about achieving apathy . . .

Herzen (*laughs*) No, I love you.

George (*hardening*) . . . which *meant*: a calming of the spirit. Apathy isn't passive, it's the freedom that comes from recognising new borders, a new country called Necessity . . . it comes from accepting that things are what they are, and not some other thing, and can't for the moment be altered . . . which people find quite difficult. We've had a terrible shock. We discovered that history has no respect for intellectuals. History is more like the weather. You never know what it's going to do. God, we were busy! – bustling about under the sky, shouting directions to the winds, remonstrating with the clouds in German, Russian, French . . . and hailing every sunbeam as proof of the power of words, some of which rhymed and scanned. Well . . . would you like to share my umbrella? It's not too bad under here. Political freedom is a rather banal ambition, after all . . . all that can't-sit-still about voting and assembling and controlling the means of production. *Stoical* freedom is nothing but not wasting your time berating the weather when it's bucketing down on your picnic.

Herzen George . . . George . . . (*to Natalie*) He's the only real Russian left in Paris. Bakunin's in Saxony under a false name – he wrote and told me! Turgenev is guess where, and Sazonov has disappeared into an aviary of

Polish conspirators who are planning a demonstration. We should go to live in . . . Italy, perhaps, or Switzerland. The best school for Kolya is in Zurich. When he's a little older my mother's going to move there to be with him.

Natalie (*to George*) They've got a new system. Put your hands on my face.

George Like that?

George touches her face lightly. Natalie stammers M's and pops P's.

Natalie Can you feel? That's how you learn if you're doing it right. Mama . . . Papa . . . Baby . . . Ball . . . George . . . George . . .

Herzen jumps up with his letter.

Herzen Ogarev's engaged to Natasha!

Natalie cries out and opens her letter. They both read.

George My wife is in an interesting condition, did I tell you?

Herzen Good for Nick!

Natalie It all started before Christmas!

George Well, it's not very interesting. In fact, it's the least interesting condition she's ever in.

Natalie I'm going to write to her this minute!

George (*vaguely*) Oh . . . all right.

Natalie Let me see what he says.

Natalie, delighted, takes Herzen's letter and gives him hers. She hurries out.

George There was always something that appealed to me about Ogarev. I don't know what it was . . . He's such a vague, lazy, hopeless sort of person. (*Pause.*) I thought he had a wife. He had a wife when I knew him in Paris.

Herzen Maria.

George Maria! She kept company with a painter, to speak loosely. Well, he applied paint to canvas and was said to have a large brush. Did she die?

Herzen No, she's alive and kicking.

George What's to be done about marriage? We should have a programme, like Proudhon. 'Property is theft, except for wives.'

Herzen Proudhon's programme of shackles from altar to coffin is an absurdity. Passions are facts. Making cages for them is the vanity of utopians, preachers, lawgivers . . . Still, passions running free, owing nothing to yesterday or tomorrow, isn't what you'd call a programme either. Ogarev is my programme. He's the only man I know who lives true to his beliefs. Fidelity is admirable, but proprietorship disgusting. But Maria was vain, flighty, I worried for Nick. She was not like my Natalie. But with Ogarev, love doesn't turn out to be pride. It's love like on the label, and he suffered it. You think that's weakness? No, it's strength.

Natalie enters wearing a hat and adjusts it, pleased, in an imaginary mirror.
Maria Ogarev, aged thirty-six, poses nude for an unseen painter.

He's a free man because he gives away freely. I'm beginning to understand the trick of freedom. Freedom can't be a residue of what was unfreely given up, divided up like a fought-over loaf. Every giving-up has to be self-willed, freely chosen, unenforceable. Each of us must

forgo only what we choose to forgo, balancing our
personal freedom of action against our need for the co-
operation of other people – who are each making the
same balance for themselves. What is the largest number
of individuals who can pull this trick off? I would say it's
smaller than a nation, smaller than the ideal communities
of Cabet or Fourier. I would say the largest number is
smaller than three. Two is possible, if there is love, but
two is not a guarantee.

APRIL 1849

*Natalie looks around. She reacts to an (imaginary)
painting. Maria enters robing herself.*

Maria I've already written to Nick . . . I told him I had
no intention of marrying again, and so had no need of a
divorce.

Natalie No . . . the need is Nick's.

Maria Exactly. Mine is to protect my position as his wife.

Natalie Your position? But, Maria, you haven't been his
wife for years now, except in name.

Maria That's a large exception, and while it's so, there's
three hundred thousand roubles in the six-per-cents,
secured against his property. Where would it leave me
if I were divorced? Worse still when there's a new wife
with her own ideas about her position. You know what
a child Nicholas is about money. Anyone can get round
him. He had four thousand souls when his father died,
and almost the first thing he did was hand over the
largest property to his serfs He's simply not someone you
can depend on. And now he sends you to plead for him
and his eager bride. Do you know her?

Natalie (*nods*) The Tuchkovs went home last year. Nick knew her before, but it was only when she returned from abroad . . . well, you know . . . and anybody would fall in love with Natasha, I fell in love with her myself!

Maria Really? Really in love?

Natalie Yes! – really, utterly, transported by love, I've never loved anyone as I loved Natasha, she brought me back to life.

Maria You were lovers?

Natalie (*in confusion*) No. What do you mean?

Maria Oh. Utterly, transportedly, but not really. Why won't you look at my picture?

Natalie Your . . .? Well . . . it seems rude to . . .

Maria You've always idealised love, and you think – surely this can't be it? (*She laughs.*) Painted from life, one afternoon when we lived in the Rue de Seine over the hat shop, do you know it? I'll take you there, we'll find something that suits you. Go on, have a good look.

Natalie (*looking*) He's got the porcelain quite well . . . What do you do with it when just anybody comes, your . . . companion's friends, the landlord, strangers . . .? Do you cover it up?

Maria No . . . it's art.

Natalie And you don't mind?

Maria shakes her head.

Maria (*confidentially*) I'm in the paint!

Natalie What do you . . . (*mean*)?

Maria Mixed in.

Natalie (*pause*) I've only been sketched in pencil.

Maria Naked?

Natalie (*laughs shyly*) Alexander doesn't draw.

Maria If an artist asks you, don't hesitate. You feel like a woman.

Natalie But I do feel like a woman, Maria. I think our sex is ennobled by idealising love. You say it as if it meant denying love in some way, but it's you who's denying it its . . . greatness . . . which comes from being a universal *idea*, like a thought in nature, without which there'd be no lovers, or artists either, because they're the same thing only happening differently and neither is any good if they deny the joined-upness of everything . . . oh dear, we should speak German for this . . .

Maria No . . . I could follow it, being in much the same state when I met Nicholas Ogarev at the Governor's Ball in Penza. A poet in exile, what could be more romantic? We sat out and talked twaddle at each other, and knew that this was love. We had no idea we were in fashion, that people who didn't know any better were falling in love quite adequately without dragging in the mind of the Universe as dreamt up by some German professor who left out the irritating details. There was also talk of the angels in heaven singing hosannas. So the next time I fell in love, it stank of turpentine, tobacco smoke, laundry baskets . . . the musk of love! To arouse and satisfy desire is nature making its point about the sexes, everything else is convention.

Natalie (*timidly*) But our animal nature is not our whole nature . . . and when the babies start coming . . .

Maria I had a child, too . . . born dead. Yes, you know, of course you know – what wouldn't Nicholas tell your

68

husband? . . . Being taken to meet Alexander for the first time was like being auditioned for my own marriage.

Natalie It was the same for me, meeting Nick, and I was expecting Sasha.

Maria Poor Nick. Even my having another man's child, it was nothing to the agony he went through when he found himself caught in the middle between his wife and his best friend.

Natalie But we all loved each other at the beginning. Don't you remember how we joined hands and knelt and thanked God for each other?

Maria Well, I didn't want to be the only one standing up.

Natalie That's not so, is it?

Maria Yes – it is so. I found it embarrassing . . . childish –

Natalie Even at the beginning! How sad for you, Maria . . . I'm sorry . . .

Maria, to Natalie's complete surprise, suddenly gives in to her rage.

Maria Don't you look down on me with your stuck-up charity, you're still the simpering little fool you always were – giving away your birthright, *idealising* it away in your prattle of exalted feelings . . . You can tell Ogarev he'll get nothing out of me, and that goes for all his friends!

The interview is evidently over. Natalie remains composed.

Natalie I'll go, then. I don't know what I said to make you angry. (*She gathers herself to leave.*) Your portrait by the way, is a failure, no doubt because your friend thinks he can produce the desired effect on canvas in the same way he produces it on you, by calculation . . . If he dips his brush here and prods it there he'll get this time what he got last time, and so on till you're done. But that's neither art nor love. You and your portrait resemble each other only in crudeness and banality. But that's a trivial failure. Imitation isn't art, everyone knows that. Technique by itself can't create. So, where do you think is the rest of the work of art if not in exalted feeling translated into paint or music or poetry, and who are you to call it prattle? German philosophy is the first time anyone's explained everything that can't be explained by the rules. Why can't your expert lover satisfy a desire to paint like Raphael or Michelangelo? That would shut me up, wouldn't it? What's stopping him? Why can't he look harder and see what the rules are? Because there aren't any. Genius isn't a matter of matching art to nature better than he can do it, it's nature itself – revealing itself through the exalted feeling of the artist, because the world isn't a collection of different things, mountains and rain and people, which have somehow landed up together, it's all one thing, like the ultimate work of art trying to reach its perfection through us, its most conscious part, and we fall short most of the time. We can't all be artists, of course, so the rest of us do the best we can at what's our consolation, we fall short at love. (*She pauses for a last look at the portrait.*) I know what it is. He's got your tits too high and your arse too small. (*Natalie leaves.*)

MAY 1849

*Saxony. In a prison room, a lawyer (Franz Otto) is
seated at a table. Bakunin is in chains, sitting opposite.*

Otto What were you doing in Dresden?

Bakunin When I arrived or when I left?

Otto Just generally.

Bakunin When I arrived I was using Dresden as my base
while plotting the destruction of the Austrian Empire.
But after a week or two, a local revolution broke out
against the King of Saxony, so I joined it.

Otto (*pause*) You understand who I am?

Bakunin Yes.

Otto I am your lawyer, nominated by the Saxon
authorities to present your defence.

Bakunin Yes.

Otto You are charged with treason, for which the
penalty is death. (*Pause.*) What brought you to Dresden?
I suspect it was to visit the art gallery with its famous
Sistine Madonna by Raphael. In all probability you had
no knowledge of any popular insurrection brewing
against the King. On May the third, when the barricades
appeared, it was a complete surprise to you.

Bakunin Yes.

Otto Ah. Good. You never planned any revolt, you had
no obligation to it or connection with it, its objectives
were of no interest to you.

Bakunin Absolutely true! The King of Saxony is welcome to dismiss his parliament as far as I'm concerned. I look on all such assemblies with contempt.

Otto There you are. At heart, you're a monarchist.

Bakunin On May the fourth I met a friend of mine in the street.

Otto Quite by chance.

Bakunin Quite by chance.

Otto His name?

Bakunin Wagner. He's a music director of the Dresden opera, at least he was till we burned it down –

Otto Er . . . don't get too far ahead.

Bakunin Oh, he was delighted – he despised the taste of the management. Anyway, Wagner said he was on his way to the Town Hall to see what was going on. So I went with him. The provisional government had just been proclaimed. They were out of their depth. The poor things hadn't the faintest idea how to conduct a revolution, so I took charge –

Otto Just – just a moment –

Bakunin The King's troops were waiting for reinforcements sent by Prussia and there was no time to be lost. I had them tear up the railway tracks, showed them where to place the cannons –

Otto Stop, stop –

Bakunin (*laughs*) There's a story that I suggested hanging the Sistine Madonna on the barricades on the theory that Prussians would be too cultured to open fire on a Raphael . . .

Otto jumps to his feet and sits again.

Otto You know who I am?

Bakunin Yes.

Otto What brought you to Dresden? Before you answer, I should tell you, both the Austrian and the Russian Emperors have asked for you to be handed over to them.

Bakunin (*pause*) When I arrived, I was using Dresden as my base while plotting the destruction of the Austrian Empire, which I consider a necessary first step to put Europe in flames and thus set off a revolution in Russia. But after a week or two, to my amazement, a revolution broke out against the King of Saxony . . .

JUNE 1849

[*From Herzen's essays*, From the Other Shore: *'Of all the suburbs of Paris I like Montmorency best. There is nothing remarkable there, no carefully trimmed parks as at St Cloud, no boudoirs of trees as at Trianon . . . In Montmorency nature is extremely simple . . . There is a large grove there, situated high up, and quiet . . . I do not know why but this grove always reminds me of our Russian woods . . . one thinks that in a minute a whiff of smoke will drift across from the byres . . . The road cuts through a clearing, and I then feel sad because instead of Zvenigorod, I see Paris . . . A small cottage with no more than three windows . . . is Rousseau's house . . .'*]

'Déjeuner sur l'herbe' . . . There is a tableau which anticipates – by fourteen years – the painting by Manet. Natalie is the undressed woman sitting on the grass in the company of two fully clothed men, George and

Herzen. Emma, stooping to pick a flower, is the woman in the background. The broader composition includes Turgenev, who is at first glance sketching Natalie but in fact sketching Emma. The tableau, however, is an overlapping of two locations, Natalie and George being in one, while Herzen, Emma and Turgenev are together elsewhere. Emma is heavily pregnant. There is a small basket near Natalie.

Herzen I let Sazonov talk me into joining his march. A few hours in custody has left me with no desire to be locked up in the Conciergerie with hundreds of prisoners and a slop bucket. I've borrowed a Wallachian passport. What we should do is take a house together, our two families across the frontier . . .

George Can I open?

Natalie Not yet.

Turgenev The police aren't interested in stopping you.

Herzen I'm not going to stay to find out like Bakunin in Saxony.

Turgenev But this is a republic.

Herzen The Crimson Cockatoo has already left for Geneva.

Natalie Are you peeping?

George No – tight shut. What are you doing?

Herzen Can I look?

Turgenev If you want.

Natalie All right, then – you can open now.

Herzen (*looking over Turgenev's shoulder*) Ah . . .

George Oh, my God!

74

Emma I have to move – I'm sorry –!

George Natalie . . .

Turgenev Of course! Move!

Natalie Sssh . . .

Turgenev I'm so sorry –

George My dear . . .

Turgenev I don't need you any more.

Emma Terrible words! . . .

George But suppose somebody . . .

Natalie Sssh . . .

Herzen He's doing clouds. I wonder what Russian modern art would be like.

Natalie I wanted to be naked for you, you see.

George I do. I do see.

Emma Where've they got to, I wonder?

Natalie Just once!

Turgenev They're hunting mushrooms.

Natalie So, when I'm sitting across from you in the objective world, listening to Alexander reading Schiller in the evenings – or picnicking at Montmorency! – you'll remember there is an inner reality, my existence-in-itself, where my naked soul is one with yours!

George I am deeply . . . Just once?

Herzen What would it be *like*?

Natalie Let's not talk . . . let's close our eyes and commune with the spirit of Rousseau among the woods where he walked!

Herzen That's where Rousseau lived, that cottage. Montmorency is the only bit of country round Paris which reminds me of Russia. Nature here is simple, not like the park at St Cloud, which is somebody's master-piece, or the disciplinarian planting at Trianon. How is the country where you go to stay?

Turgenev Delightful.

Emma Do your friends have land?

Turgenev It wouldn't count for much at home. You can see right across it.

Herzen How many souls do they have?

Turgenev One each.

Natalie Oh, George! I ask for nothing but to give!

George Please get dressed before . . .

Natalie I ask nothing of you but to take!

George I will, I will, but not here . . .

Natalie To take strength from me.

George Oh, yes, yes, you're the only one who understands me.

Herzen Well, what do you do there?

Turgenev We like to go out shooting.

Herzen Madame Viardot shoots?

Turgenev No, she's not an American, she's an opera singer. Her husband shoots.

Herzen Ah. Is he accurate?

Turgenev crumples up his drawing.

Emma Oh – what a waste of being still.

George But Emma must be wondering . . .

Natalie Let's tell her!

George No!

Natalie Why ever not?

George Besides, she'd tell Alexander.

Natalie Do you think so? Alexander must never know.

George I agree.

Natalie He wouldn't understand.

George No, he wouldn't

Natalie If only he could see there's no egoism in my love.

George We'll find a way.

Natalie One day, perhaps . . .

George Yes, let me think – Tuesday . . .

Natalie But until then . . .

George Yes – so put your clothes on, my dear spirit, my beautiful soul!

Natalie Don't look, then.

George Oh God, we haven't found a single mushroom!

George snatches up the basket, and hurries away.
Natalie starts getting dressed.

Turgenev (*to Herzen*) You still own a small estate at home, I believe. How many souls do *you* have?

Herzen None now. The government took it. But you're quite right. I apologise.

Turgenev I freed my mother's household serfs, with land, but I receive quit-rent from the rest.

Emma Honestly, you Russians.

Herzen I'm going to find George and Natalie. (*Herzen leaves.*)

Emma What are you writing now?

Turgenev A play.

Emma Is it about us?

Turgenev It takes place over a month in a house in the country. A woman and a young girl fall in love with the same man.

Emma Who wins?

Turgenev Nobody, of course.

Emma I want to ask you something but you might be angry with me.

Turgenev I'll answer anyway. No.

Emma But how do you know the question?

Turgenev I don't. You can apply my answer to any question of your choice.

Emma That's a good system . . . Well, I'm sorry. Devotion such as yours should not go unrewarded.

Pause.

Emma Now I want to ask you something else.

Turgenev Yes.

Emma starts to weep.

I'm sorry.

Emma But you're right. If you knew how I suffer. George was my first.

78

Turgenev My first was a serf. I think my mother put her up to it. I was fifteen. I was in the garden. It was a drizzly sort of day. Suddenly I saw a girl coming towards me . . . she came right to me. I was her master, you must remember. She was my slave. She took hold of me by the hair and said, 'Come!' . . . Unforgettable . . . Words stagger after. Art despairs.

Emma That's different. That's eroticism.

Turgenev Yes.

Emma Have you ever been happy?

Turgenev But I have moments of extreme happiness . . . ecstasy! –

Emma Do you?

Turgenev – watching a duck scratching the back of its head with that quick back-and-forth of its damp foot . . . and the way slow silver threads of water stream from a cow's mouth when it raises its head from the edge of the pond to stare at you . . .

Herzen enters.

Herzen Rousseau has a lot to answer for.

George follows Herzen, with the basket.

George Oh . . . why do you say that?

Natalie leaves. Emma takes the basket and upends it. A single virulent toadstool falls out.

Herzen I idolised Rousseau when I was young . . . Man in his natural state, uncorrupted by civilisation, desiring only those things which are good to desire . . .

George Oh, yes.

Herzen . . . and everybody free to follow their desires without conflicts because they'd all want the same things . . .

Emma Where's Natalie?

George Didn't she come back?

Herzen She'll be rounding up the nurse and the children.

George (*to Emma*) My love, what do you think? We're going to share a house with Alexander and Natalie in Nice! He's going to go on ahead and find a place.

Emma Why . . . why leave Paris?

Herzen We belong to Egypt, not to the Promised Land. The people faltered. I wouldn't insult them by absolving them. They had no programme, and no sovereign brain to carry one out. The Sovereign People are our invention. The masses are more like a phenomenon in nature, and nature isn't interested in our fantasy that ink is action. Ask George. We're dupes.

Natalie enters.

(*to Natalie*) I'm a dupe. Well and good. We, too, will look to our faults – our passions and vices – and prepare ourselves by living by our ideals in a republic of our own. We are many! – Nine, counting my mother and the children.

Natalie The children must be hungry. I'm starving.

Turgenev It's going to rain.

Herzen (*to Natalie*) George has offered to escort you and the children on your journey south. (*to Emma*) Your husband is kindness itself.

George (*to Emma*) And when you've had the baby, you'll join us.

Emma (*to Herzen*) There's nothing he wouldn't do for you.

Natalie Come on – we can go in that empty cottage.

Herzen and Natalie leave, holding hands.

George (*to Turgenev*) Are you writing anything?

Turgenev Well . . . no . . .

Emma Yes, he is. It's a comedy.

Turgenev Here it comes.

Turgenev puts his palm out to the first drops. They leave, following Herzen and Natalie.

SEPTEMBER 1850

Nice (at this time an Italian town).
Herzen is writing on the verandah of a large house on the Promenade. The light is Mediterranean, the sea washing the shingles is audible, part of the garden is visible. The verandah is a large area containing a family dining table and chairs, and some comfortable chairs around a smaller table. There is a door to the interior.
Mother and Kolya are absorbed together, at a distance from Herzen, using a hand mirror (in which Kolya studies his mouth movements). An Italian servant, Rocca, is laying the table and singing for his own enjoyment. As he goes indoors, he passingly 'serenades' Mother and Kolya. Mother manages a game smile. With her collusion, Kolya trots over to Herzen. Herzen slightly over-enunciates for Kolya.

Herzen *Was moechtest du denn?* [*What do you want, darling?*]

Kolya looks back to Mother for assurance. She smiles him on.

Kolya *Ich spreche Russisch!* [*I speak Russian!*] (*in 'English'*) 'Sunny day! My name is Kolya!'

Herzen *Wunderbar!* [*Wonderful!*]

Great delight, made physical, on all sides.

Jetzt sprichst du Russisch! [*Now you speak Russian!*]

Kolya *Ich spreche Russisch!* [*I speak Russian!*]

Rocca returns, singing, with more things for the table.

Herzen *Zeig es Mami!* [*Show Mummy!*] *Do vei Signora?* [*Where is the Signora?*]

Rocca *Sta nel giardino.* [*She was in the garden.*]

Rocca leaves singing.

Mother I suppose the next one will juggle.

Herzen places Kolya's hands on Herzen's face and enunciates while Kolya lip-reads.

Herzen (*to Kolya*) *Garten.* [*Garden.*]

Kolya trots off out of sight.

Mother But Italy is friendlier than Switzerland, especially to children and old ladies. The school in Zurich was the last straw – what a shock when they discovered they were harbouring the child of a dangerous revolutionary instead of a Russian nobleman.

Herzen I was pleased that my little book made such an impression on the good burghers of Zurich . . . and we stole the school's best teacher for Kolya, so it's ended well – (*He looks at his watch.*) – and I have to meet him off the diligence at Genoa. He'll soon have Kolya orating on the seashore like Demosthenes with a pebble in his mouth. But I want you to be happy here, too.

Mother I, too? (*She kisses him.*)

Herzen I liked Nice when we came through here on our way to Rome three years ago, do you remember?

Mother I remember the shingle beach when we were on our way back after the French Republic was declared . . . and the excitement, when we reached the border, of having Republican stamps in our passports . . . A French stamp, even before the Republic, would get you into trouble at home, Sasha . . .

Herzen How can I go back? I've tried suffocation, darkness, fear and censorship – and I've tried air, light, security and freedom to publish – and I know which is better. There's no emperor or king or pope in Europe who can match the Tsar for despotism, especially now after the almighty scare he got . . . The people here have had a civilisation for two thousand years, and they keep something of themselves which no passing tyranny can eradicate. But I'll show you why I can't go home again. (*He goes to the table where he has been working and picks up a French journal.*) Here's a man writing about us. It's a French paper. He's the first person in France to write about the Russian people, and he can prove that the Russian people are not human, because they are devoid of moral sense. The Russian is a thief and a liar, and is so innocently because it's his nature.

Mother He doesn't mean us, he means the peasants.

Herzen Yes, they lie to landowners, officials, judges, policemen . . . and steal from them – and they are right because they are denied every kind of self-protection and dignity. What have our moral categories got to do with the Russians we've abandoned? Not to steal would be to

83

concede the fairness of their portion. For two hundred years their whole life has been one long dumb passive protest against the existing order. They have no one to speak for them.

Mother What time is the diligence?

Herzen God give me Medea!

Mother (*indicating the garden*) Kolya's nagging Natalie to go to the beach – and she's in no fit state – where's the nurse?

Herzen (*throwing down the journal*) This is not some demented pamphleteer, he's a distinguished historian famous for his humanitarian views, writing for intelligent Frenchmen – (*shouting after her*) It's about time to acquaint Europe with Russia, don't you think?

> *Mother leaves.*
> *Herzen looks at his watch, hurries away, reverses direction and shouts towards the garden.*

Don't let go of his hand in the water!

> *Leaving again, he encounters Emma, who is no longer pregnant, wheeling a small baby carriage.*

Is there any news of George? When is he coming?

Emma I don't know.

Herzen Well, it's too bad of him. We're not complete without him.

> *Natalie, seven months pregnant, comes into view.*

(*to Natalie*) I'm going to pick up Spielmann. That's his name! – Spielmann!

> *Laughing, he runs off calling for Rocca. Natalie comes forward.*

84

Natalie Was there a letter?

Emma gives Natalie a sealed letter.

Thank you. (*Natalie puts the letter in her bosom.*)

Emma If he says when he's coming, perhaps you'll tell me.

Natalie Yes, of course.

Emma If you loved him, you'd leave Alexander.

Natalie (*shakes her head*) Alexander must be spared this. The one time he began to wonder . . . he nearly lost his mind. I would have done anything to reassure him.

Emma You did the simplest thing. If you weren't in a state where you can hardly be said to be of practical use, George would be here now.

Natalie You mustn't humiliate yourself, Emma. He loves you, too.

Emma I'm a post office, and living upstairs in your house like a lodger, which is all we can afford to be – there is no further humiliation I could suffer. But I'm glad to do it for my George. He was unrecognisable when I came from Paris. He was suffering more than I. If you can't make him happy – or cure him – give him back. He'll come back anyway. This is not love, it's exaltation.

Emma's baby starts crying. She picks it up, and paces.

Natalie You haven't understood anything. All my actions spring from the divine spirit of love, which I feel for all creation. Your logical way of looking at things just shows that you have grown apart from Nature. George is not the way you talk about him. He understands. He loves you. He loves Alexander. He loves your children

85

and mine. Together, our love will be strong enough for all of us.

George enters, in travelling clothes. He takes one look at his wife, baby and pregnant mistress, and turns about.

Natalie George!

Emma George!

Natalie, with a glad cry runs after him, followed by Emma.

NOVEMBER 1850

A newborn baby starts squalling inside the house. Bouquets of flowers arrive, by messenger and butler (Rocca).
Herzen and George appear from indoors in smoking jackets, with cigars and glasses of champagne.

Herzen (*toasts*) To Natalie and baby Olga.

George To Natalie and Olga.

Herzen Where's Emma?

George looks around.

George There.

DECEMBER 1850

The same place. A Nurse (Maria Fomm) wheels a smart pram. Emma is holding her crying eighteen-month-old child and close to hysteria. Herzen is writing what turns out to be a cheque and an IOU. When the baby raises

its voice, Emma continues louder, so the decibel level
threatens sometimes to become ludicrous.

Emma On our honeymoon in Italy George didn't like
the cologne they had there, so I sent to Paris for his
special cologne and when it arrived in Rome we were
in Naples, and when it reached Naples we were back
in Rome, and so it went on until the cologne followed
us back to Paris. The carriage charges were enormous.
That's how I've always been with George. Nothing
was too good or too much. Daddy used to be rich, he
supplied all the silk furnishings to the Prussian court,
but somehow the revolution made him quite poor and
he resents George, it's so unfair. I've borrowed and sold
everything I can so that George isn't troubled, and now
I don't know where else to turn.

> *Natalie, no longer pregnant, wearing white, is seen*
> *being painted in Mediterranean sunshine.*

I felt you would be sympathetic because Natalie and
I have such a close bond in George. He hardly wrote to
me in all the months I was left behind in Paris. Natalie is
the one who wrote, to tell me how wonderful and kind
and sensitive George is, how good with your children,
how adorable he is . . . She has such a broad loving
heart, there's room for everybody in it, it seems . . .

Herzen (*giving her the cheque*) Ten thousand francs for
two years.

> *She signs the receipt, takes the cheque and leaves, with*
> *her crying baby.*

JANUARY 1851

Natalie, with the painting she posed for, comes to show it to Herzen.

Herzen Oh yes . . . Where will we put it?

Natalie Oh . . . but it's a present for George for the New Year.

Herzen How silly of me.

Natalie Do you like it?

Herzen Very much. If Herwegh will permit it, I'll order a copy made for myself.

Natalie You're angry.

Herzen What should I have to be angry about?

Natalie Take it for yourself, then.

Herzen Nothing would induce me.

Natalie becomes tearful and confused.

Natalie George is like my child. He becomes distressed – destroyed – or elated – by the smallest things. You're a grown man among men, you don't understand the yearning for love of a sensitive being for a different kind of love –

Herzen Please speak plainly.

Natalie He worships you, he lives for your approval, spare him this –

Herzen Natalie, examine your heart calmly, be open with yourself, and with me. If you want me to go, I'll go – I'll go to America with Sasha –

Natalie becomes almost hysterical.

Natalie How can you! How can you! As though such a thing were possible! You're my homeland, my whole life. I've lived on my love for you as in God's world, without it I wouldn't exist, I'd have to be born again to have a life at all –

Herzen Plain speech for God's sake! Has Herwegh – known you?

Natalie If only you could understand! – you would beg my forgiveness for what you're saying.

Herzen Has he taken you?

Natalie I have taken him – to my bosom like a babe.

Herzen Is this poetry or infantilism? I want to know if he's your lover.

Natalie I am pure before myself and before the world – I bear no reproach in the very depths of my heart – now you know.

Herzen (*exasperated*) Now I know what?

Natalie That I am yours, that I love you, that my affection for George is God-given – if he went away I would sicken – if you went away, I would die! Perhaps *I* should be the one to go – to Russia for a year – Natasha is the only one who would understand the purity of my love. Oh, how did this happen? How did this innocent world of my loving heart shatter to fragments?

Herzen Christ! Just tell me without the doubletalk! – Is Herwegh your lover?!

Natalie He loves me, yes – he loves me –

Herzen Is he your lover? Have you been to his bed?

Natalie Oh – I see. You have no objection if I take him to my heart, only to my bed –

Herzen Precisely. Or his bed, or a flowerbed, or up against the back of the town hall –

Natalie Alexander, Alexander, this is not you, this is not the great-hearted soul I gave my tender innocent heart to when I –

Herzen shakes her.

Herzen Tell me, damn your speeches! Is it true?

Natalie collapses weeping.

It's true, then. Say it. Say it.

Natalie He is my lover! There!

Herzen Thank you. That guttersnipe – that unctuous, treacherous, lecher – that *thief*! –

Natalie Oh my God, what have we done – and the children!

Herzen There was a time to think of that before you besmirched all of us with your common little fall from grace – well, I shall go!

Natalie No – no! – It'll kill him!

Herzen Kill *him*? What kind of mockery of a love affair is this?

Natalie I swear it – he'll kill himself. He's got a pistol.

Herzen laughs madly.

Herzen Well, he'd better clean it if it's the one he went to war with – the barrel must be full of mud!

Natalie Alexander, aren't you ashamed? I'm at your mercy and you make a joke of a love which gave me back my life.

Herzen Oh – thank you! Thank you! And what was your life before I took you from it in the clothes you stood up in?

Natalie It was wretched. You're right. I gave it to you joyfully, it belongs to you to do what you want with, so kill me all at once and not little by little!

Natalie collapses sobbing. Herzen sits next to her and takes her hands, his fury spent.

Herzen And you forgot to bring your hat. (*He gives way to tears, embracing her.*) Forgive me, too – forgive everything I said. They are not things I believe. I have lost something I hardly gave a thought to. My existence. My purchase on my life.

Emma enters.

Emma George wants you to kill him.

Herzen laughs.

Herzen Can't he ask me himself?

Emma This is a calamity for both of us, but compare your behaviour with mine. Let Natalie go away with him.

Herzen Of course! If she wants to.

Emma goes to Natalie and kneels by her.

Emma Save him.

Natalie I can't. What strength I have I need for Alexander. I will go wherever he goes.

Herzen It's him who's going. (*to Emma*) I'll pay your fares to Genoa provided you leave in the morning.

Emma gets up.

Emma We can't leave. There are tradesmen's accounts we have to settle.

Herzen It will be my pleasure.

Emma runs back to Natalie and flings herself down in desperation.

Emma If you won't go with George, ask him to take me when he goes! – Ask him not to abandon me!

Herzen You're asking my wife to plead for you . . .?

Emma Will you?

Natalie nods. Emma gets up to go.

(*to Herzen*) Egoist!

Herzen But you've made yourself a slave, and this is where it's got you.

Emma leaves.

Of *course* I'm an egoist! How strange people are! – taking pride in humility . . . in servitude to others . . . and the whole system of duties designed by authority to keep us quiet and as little different from each other as possible . . . Why should we damp down everything in us which is our uniqueness, the salt of our personality . . . the tiny furnace which needs to be constantly fed with self-esteem to keep us warm and vital and, yes, of use to our brothers and neighbours? Egoism isn't an acquired vice. It's not an acquired virtue either. It's just part of what comes with being human, to keep us free, to create our own destiny, and our values. It's not the enemy of love! It's what love feeds on. That's why without you I'd be destroyed.

Herzen's self-assurance collapses. Natalie comforts him. She is altered back, and speaks as one who is dry-eyed.

Natalie No . . . no . . . You wouldn't be destroyed, Alexander. I'm only a little part of your . . . your sense of worth. I can't give it back to you. But it's not lost between us. It passes to me. I'll never leave you. But think what I have lost, too . . . the ideal of a love which is greater the more it includes, instead of more hurtful, squalid and ridiculous.

Rocca is heard – and then seen – singing. He is laying the table and making the verandah festive.

NOVEMBER 1851

Herzen is working on the verandah. Rocca, singing, is making the verandah and dining table festive, helped by a Maid. Rocca leaves and returns.

Rocca *Principe!*

Rocca admits a man who is the Russian Consul. The Consul bows. Rocca leaves.

Consul Leonty Vasilevich Ibayev. I am addressing Alexander Ivanovich Herzen, of course.

Herzen You are.

Consul I am the Russian Consul in Nice.

Herzen Good heavens.

Consul I have a communication to make to you.

Herzen From whom?

Consul From Count Orlov.

Herzen Ah. Last time, it was good news. Please sit down.

Consul Thank you.

The Consul sits down and takes a document from his pocket. He reads it out.

'Adjutant-General Count Orlov has notified Count Nesselrode, Minister of Foreign Affairs, that – (*He rises to his feet, inclining his head.*) – His Imperial Majesty – (*He sits again.*) – has been graciously pleased to order that Alexander Ivanovich Herzen shall return to Russia at once – of which he is to be informed, accepting from him no reasons for delay and granting him no postponement under any circumstances.' (*He folds the document and puts it in his pocket.*) What am I to answer?

Herzen That I'm not going.

Consul How do you mean, 'not going'?

Herzen Just that. Not going. Remaining. Staying put.

Consul You don't understand. His Imperial – (*He stands, bows his head, and sits.*) – Majesty is ordering you . . .

Herzen Yes, and I'm not going.

Consul You mean, you are humbly requesting a delay in the execution of the will of His Imperial –

Herzen No, no, I can't make myself any clearer. I'm not asking for a delay. I'm not going at any time.

Consul An indefinite delay, you mean? You are ill, perhaps, too ill to travel. There would be precedents for that.

Herzen One of us is mad. I'm in excellent health, especially mental health, so it must be you. Do you really think I would hold out my wrists for the handcuffs on the say-so of His Imperial – sit down, for God's sake!

Consul But what am I to do? Look on it from my position. If I were to be the intermediary for an act of disobedience to the will of His Imp – (*He starts to rise but checks himself.*) – Majesty, it would call attention to my name in a most unfavourable context. It might even look as if I'm giving myself airs . . . being privy to something so inimicable to His Majesty's dignity, so incommensurable with the vastness of his anger, before which nations tremble.

Herzen (*amused now*) I see what you mean.

Consul Thank you.

Herzen But it would be Count Orlov to whom you'd be giving the bad news.

Consul It's the same thing. Count Orlov would never forget my name.

Herzen But you're only the messenger.

Consul There's a streak of the Cleopatra in him.

Herzen We'd better have a drink. Rocca! Vino.

   Rocca interrupts an aria, to serve the wine.

Why don't I write personally to Count Orlov? Then you wouldn't know what I've said.

Consul Would you do that? I'd be immensely grateful.

   Herzen starts writing. The wine is served.

Are you having a celebration?

Herzen A homecoming. My mother has been in Paris with one of my children. They're returning tonight on the Marseilles steamer.

Consul Your little boy who is deaf?

95

Herzen I was *wondering* why Orlov would keep a consul in a place like this.

Consul No, no . . . what an egoist! I see your children with their nurse, playing on the beach. But you're right. Life is very quiet. Very few passports are being issued to travellers since the . . . events in Europe.

Natalie comes on to the verandah with Sazonov.

Natalie Look who's come from Geneva!

Herzen (*to the Consul*) Allow me to present you to my wife. This is Mr . . .

Consul Ibayev, Russian Consul.

Natalie is frightened.

Natalie What . . .? (*to Herzen*) Is everything all right?

Herzen Perfectly. (*to the Consul*) And this is . . .

Sazonov becomes suave.

Sazonov Ah. I'm impressed. I never told anyone I was coming.

Consul I had business with Mr Herzen.

Sazonov laughs sceptically.

Sazonov Of course. Please compliment Count Orlov for me . . . on his excellent information.

Consul Do you know Count Orlov?

Sazonov No. But I dare say he knows me. I was a thorn in his side for many years in Paris.

Herzen Sit down, have a drink –

Sazonov (*ignoring Herzen*) No doubt you know a little bit about my . . . activities in Geneva. Tell Orlov we will undoubtedly be meeting one day.

Consul Certainly. What name shall I say?

Sazonov Just say . . . the blue nightingale is still flying in the sky . . . He'll understand.

Herzen signs and seals the letter.

Herzen All done.

The Consul accepts the letter and bows to Natalie and Sazonov. Herzen accompanies him out.
    There is a transition to evening.
    Natalie and Rocca, perhaps with a maid, are completing the preparations for the reunion, with Chinese lanterns, bunting, toys on the table, and a 'Welcome Kolya' sign. (In an ideal world Sasha would be part of this, but he is eleven now. His never-seen sister, Tata, would be seven.)
    Sazonov is vaguely helping, too, but soon gives up to ramble on and drink. Natalie hardly bothers to listen to him.

Sazonov I've had a letter from Botkin . . . Alexander's pamphlet on the development of revolutionary ideas in Russia gave heart attacks to his friends in the Moscow University circle . . . (*He becomes conscious of Rocca, and suddenly addresses him.*) Watch out, look what you're doing!

Rocca reacts late and baffled.

Natalie He doesn't know Russian. He's our Italian servant. (*to Rocca*) E niente. [*It's nothing.*]

Sazonov You can't be too careful.

Natalie Why aren't they here yet? I should have gone with Alexander to meet the steamer . . .

Sazonov What else . . .? Moscow was *en fête* for the opening of the railway. Tsar Nicholas loves it. He inspected every bridge and tunnel personally. His German relatives impressed everyone by their appetites in the station refreshment room . . .

Natalie (*distracted*) Why are they so late? It's probably Granny's trunks. She travels like an archduchess.

Sazonov Who's with them?

Natalie Only her maid, I think, and Spielmann, Kolya's tutor. (*to Rocca*) *Por favor, vai a vedere se vengano.* [*Please go and see if they're coming.*]

Sazonov The speech man? Are you mad? That can't be his real name!

Rocca meets Herzen at the edge of the stage. Herzen brushes past him. Natalie sees him.

Natalie Alexander . . .? Where are they?

Herzen They're not coming. The boat from Marseilles . . . isn't coming.

Herzen embraces her, weeping.

Natalie (*bewildered*) They're not coming at all?

Herzen No. There was an accident at sea . . . Oh, Natalie!

Natalie When is Kolya coming?

Herzen He's never coming. I'm sorry.

Natalie fights out of his embrace and pummels him.

Natalie Don't you dare tell me that! (*She runs inside.*)

Herzen (*to Rocca*) Get rid of everything. (*Herzen gestures at the decorations.*)

Sazonov God . . . what happened?

Herzen They got rammed by another boat. A hundred people drowned. (*to Rocca in Italian*) Get rid of all this.

Herzen follows Natalie indoors. She starts to howl in her grief. Rocca uncertainly starts to blow out the candles.

AUGUST 1852

At night Herzen stands by the guard rail on the deck of the cross-Channel steamer at sea. After a few moments he realises that Bakunin is at the rail, too.

Bakunin Where are we off to? Who's got the map?

Herzen Michael? Are you dead?

Bakunin No.

Herzen That's good. I was just thinking about you and there you are, how very . . . un-odd! – yes, looking just like you looked when I saw you off in the rain on the tender to Kronstadt where the steamer was waiting. Do you remember?

Bakunin You were the only one who came to see me off.

Herzen And now you're the only one who's come to see *me* off!

Bakunin Where are you going?

Herzen England.

Bakunin Alone?

Herzen Natalie died, three months ago . . . We lost Kolya. He was drowned at sea, my mother with him, and a young man who was teaching Kolya to speak. None of them was ever found. It finished my Natalie.

She was expecting another baby, and when it came she had no strength left. The baby died, too.

Bakunin My poor friend.

Herzen Oh, Michael, you should have heard Kolya talk! He had such a funny, charming way . . . and he understood everything you said, you'd swear he was listening! The thing I can't bear . . . (*He almost breaks down.*) . . . I just wish it hadn't happened at night. He couldn't hear in the dark. He couldn't see your lips.

Bakunin Little Kolya, his life cut so short! Who is this Moloch . . . ?

Herzen No, no, not at all! His life was what it was. Because children grow up, we think a child's purpose is to grow up. But a child's purpose is to be a child. Nature doesn't disdain what lives only for a *day*. It pours the whole of itself into the each moment. We don't value the lily less for not being made of flint and built to last. Life's bounty is in its flow, later is too late. Where is the song when it's been sung? The dance when it's been danced? It's only we humans who want to own the future, too. We persuade ourselves that the universe is modestly employed in unfolding our destination. We note the haphazard chaos of history by the day, by the hour, but there is something wrong with the picture. Where is the unity, the meaning, of nature's highest creation? Surely those millions of little streams of accident and wilfulness have their correction in the vast underground river which, without a doubt, is carrying us to the place where we're expected! But there is no such place, that's why it's called utopia. The death of a child has no more meaning than the death of armies, of nations. Was the child happy while he lived? That is a proper question, the only question. If we can't arrange our own happiness, it's a conceit beyond vulgarity to arrange the

100

happiness of those who come after us. (*Pause.*) What happened to you, Michael? Were you betrayed?

Bakunin No. I ran out of revolutions. When the soldiers caught up with me, I was too tired to care. I only wanted to sleep. I had plenty of time to sleep after that . . . nine months in fetters in the fortress of Königstein, and, when the Germans had done with me, as long again in Prague Castle. Thank you for the money you sent. I was allowed to order cigars and books. I learned English! (*accented*) 'George and Mary go to the seaside.' How is George? Thank him for me. Emma sent a hundred francs, too. Small sums of money came from democrats all over, from people I didn't know. Brotherhood before bread, it's not all bathwater.

Herzen You've become a myth. I heard that society ladies were collecting funds for a rescue attempt.

Bakunin Word must have got back to Russia – there were twenty Cossacks waiting at the border to escort me to the Peter and Paul Fortress. No, it's up to the revolution now.

Herzen What revolution?

Bakunin The Russian revolution. It can't be long coming now. Our Westerniser friends at home were waiting for a Russian bourgeoisie to make a revolution for their children, but – don't you see? – *not* having a bourgeoisie is Russia's good fortune!

Herzen Don't tell me, tell them.

Bakunin Our own revolution, Herzen! Not a bourgeois revolution like in Europe – they let us down very badly, the Germans and the French, they were all for getting rid of aristocratic privilege, but they closed ranks to defend their property.

Herzen What did you expect?

Bakunin Well, why didn't you tell me?

Herzen You never listened.

Bakunin Why should I listen? There were more *poor* people with the vote than *rich* people . . . How could it turn out the way it did?

Herzen It's as Proudhon said, universal suffrage is counter-revolutionary.

Bakunin He kept coming out with those, Pierre-Joseph, didn't he? I taught him Hegel. His wife would serve supper by the fire, go to bed, get up, and serve breakfast, and we'd still be sat there over the embers, going through the categories . . . Great days, Herzen!

Herzen Oh . . . Bakunin!

Bakunin We were there for the February revolution. It was the happiest time of my life.

Herzen I was in Italy. Ten days after I got back to Paris, I knew the revolution was dead . . . and now the Republic is dead, too. *Vive la mort!* Did you know? President Louis-Napoleon turned himself into Emperor Louis-Napoleon with only a few thousand arrests. People didn't care. It was one way out of a Republic which was ashamed of itself. The Second Empire arrived just in time to finish the year off nicely. Expect important changes in furniture and ladies' fashions. You're right. It's over with us Russians and the western model. Civilisation passed us by, we belonged to geography, not history, so we escaped. We can now get on without being distracted. The West has nothing to teach us. It's sinking under its weight of precious cargo which it won't jettison – all those shackles for the mind. With us it's all ballast. Over the side with it! We're too oppressed to make do with half-liberty. We're free to act because we have nothing.

Bakunin I couldn't wait to get to the West! Twenty Cossacks couldn't have held me back in my yearning for the other shore. But the answer was behind me all the time. A peasant revolution, Herzen! Marx bamboozled us. He's such a townie, to him peasants are hardly people, they're agriculture, like cows and turnips. Well, he doesn't know the Russian peasant! There's a history of rebellion there, and we forgot it.

Herzen Stop – stop . . .

Bakunin I don't mean your hand-kissing, priest-fearing greybeards – the Slavophils can have those. I mean men and women who are ready to burn everything in sight and string up the landlord! – with policemen's heads on their pitchforks!

Herzen Stop! – 'Destruction is a creative passion!' You're such a . . . *child*! We have to go to the people, bring them with us, step by step. But Russia has a chance. The village commune can be the foundation of true populism, not Aksakov's sentimental paternalism, and not the iron bureaucracy of a socialist elite, but self-government from the ground up. Russian socialism! After the farce of 1848, I was in despair. My life meant nothing. Russia saved me . . . and then fate had another trick up its sleeve . . . Are you there, Michael?

Bakunin Oh, yes. If it goes your way, I'll be there for years. (*Bakunin leaves.*)

Herzen Nobody's got the map. In the West, socialism may win next time, but it's not history's destination. Socialism, too, will reach its own extremes and absurdities, and once more Europe will burst at the seams. Borders will change, nationalities break up, cities burn . . . the collapse of law, education, manufacture, fields left to rot – military rule and money in flight to England, America . . . And then a new war will begin between the barefoot and the shod. It will be bloody, swift and unjust, and leave Europe like Bohemia after the Hussites. Are you sorry for civilisation? I am sorry for it, too.

Natalie's voice – from the past – is heard distantly calling repeatedly for Kolya. Distant thunder.

He can't hear you. I'm sorry. I'm so sorry, Natalie.

SUMMER 1846

Sokolovo as before: a continuation. Distant thunder.
Sasha continues putting the fallen mushrooms into the basket.
Natalie's voice is still calling for Kolya. Sasha stops to look and listen. Men's voices can be heard yet more distantly, calling to each other – i.e., Herzen and his friends directing each other in the search. Ogarev enters, calling to Natalie.

Ogarev Kolya's here! He's with me.

Natalie (*entering*) Oh, thank God . . . thank God!

Ogarev No panic, no panic . . . he followed the ditch, he's filthy.

Natalie runs across.

Natalie (*offstage*) Mummy thought she'd lost you! Come on, let's wash you in the stream. (*receding*) Alexander! . . . Here! . . .

Ogarev still has Sasha's fishing cane and jam jar. Distantly, the men are heard shouting to each other, calling off the search. A final distant sound of thunder.

Life, life . . . (*to Sasha*) I got to know your papa because
of a man nearly drowning . . . in the river at Luzhniki.

Sasha (*interested*) Really?

Ogarev Yes, really! A Cossack who was grazing his horse
on the Sparrow Hills came running down into the water
and saved him, a real hero! Your father was playing by
the river and saw it all, and he told his papa, who wrote
to the Cossack's commanding officer about it. The man
who was saved came to your house to thank your
grandpa for doing that, and so he became friends with
your family. And where do I come in? Well, the man in
the water later became my tutor, and one day when I was
about twelve years old, he took me to meet a boy he'd
come to know because of being nearly drowned, and
that's how I met your daddy, and we became best
friends.

Sasha No, you're not, I don't know you.

Ogarev Why, I patted your behind before you were
born! It was the happiest day of my life, that day. We
knelt down together, holding hands, your mother and
father and my wife and I, and . . . But you're right, later
I went travelling. (*Pause.*) No, my *happiest* day was
another day, before that, up on the Sparrow Hills, just
where the Cossack had come running down, and your
daddy and I . . . we climbed up to the top where the sun
was setting on Moscow spread out below us, and we
made a promise to . . . to be revolutionaries together.
I was thirteen then. (*He gives a little laugh and looks up.*)
The storm has missed us.

Herzen (*off stage*) Nick . . . !

 Herzen enters with the letter from Orlov.

Ogarev Tell Sasha who I am.

Herzen Look . . . from Count Orlov.

He gives the letter to Ogarev, who starts to read it.

(*to Sasha*) Nick? Nick is my best friend.

Ogarev returns the letter to Herzen.

Ogarev (*to Sasha*) See?

Ogarev embraces Herzen in joyous congratulation.
Natalie enters.
A slow fade begins.
Servants enter to clear up the coffee tray, etc.
Ogarev, Herzen, Natalie and Sasha stroll away
towards the house, taking the basket of mushrooms.